LIVING A RESURRECTED LIFE

New Edition

GOD IS IN US FOR US

LIVING A

RESURRECTED LIFE

HEAVENLY LIFE EXPERIENCE ON EARTH

MELUSI T NTOMBELA

MT Mystery

Living A Resurrected Life

By Melusi T Ntombela

Copyright © 2021 by Melusi T Ntombela

ISBN: 978-1-7762-8254-8

Unless otherwise indicated, all Scriptures quotations are taken from KJV® Bible (The Holy Bible: King James Version®)

Available in eBook and paperback,

Cover design: Sibusiso Mabuza of SBU Design

Some of the names and details of people referenced in this book have been hid to protect the privacy of those involved.

CONTENTS

ACKNOWLEDGMENTS

First, to Christ Jesus, "I thank You for allocating Your grace for me, even when I was far from perfection You entrusted me with the mysteries of the kingdom of God. You hold me by hand and lead me into Your inner presence. You allow me to experience Your unlimited power and endless glory, with no doubts You have forever cleared my salvation. My life is Yours and I shall forever praise You.

Second, to Lindo Fortunate Chirwa, when everyone expected me to be always strong and have all possible solutions to every problem, you knew my pain and weaknesses. You always encourage me to be the better version of myself and for that I will never stop thanking you.

Thirdly, Bishop KN and the first lardy MV Mnisi, in my trying moments and rejection, you stood your ground and believed in me even when I never truly knew what I was becoming. And that was reason enough for me to keep pushing for better.

Fourthly, to all the family, friends and partners of MT Mystery Ministries and Age Of Greater Glory International Ministries; it's one thing to be anointed and it's a complete different thing to have people believing in you and ready to support you all the way through. Thank you for standing with me and supporting me in spreading the gospel of Jesus Christ with love across the nations.

Finally, to all those who have made it possible for this book to be published and all our supporters, you're all greatly appreciated.

DEDICATION

THIS BOOK IS DEDICATED TO A GROUP OF INDIVIDUALS CALLED "THE TEAM OF FIRE". YOU ALL HAVE BEEN CAREFULLY HAND CHOSEN BY GOD AS A GIFT TO OUR GENERATION. I KNOW THE DEVIL HAS REALLY FOUGHT YOUR RISING, BUT PLEASE IN WHATSOEVER YOU DO WHEREVER YOU ARE; JUST NEVER FORGET WHO AND WHAT YOU ARE.

Therefore, we are buried with him by baptism into death: that like as Christ was raised up from the dead by the glory of the Father, even so we also should walk in newness of like.

Romans 6:4

GOD IS IN US FOR US

INTRODUCTION

"LIFE" What is LIFE? With all the intelligence of human's wisdom we have never really found a common definition of life apart from explaining it through situations and experiences. Maybe, it might be because we have tried explaining life without involving God.

Having things that we socialize with on our daily experiences yet still we can't fully comprehend or understand, it is proving we must accept that there is a supreme ONE who governs above all.

In as much as we all defines life differently, there has to be the origin of life which will then bring us into a common understanding of life. Accepting the supremacy of God comes with understanding that He is the primal origin of existence which makes Him to be Life and without Him there is no life at all. If we are to reduce life into just breath and our daily social experiences, then we have not mastered the true nature of life and its power to our everyday experiences.

Life is the ability to trap God and express Him to all nature. If we can master the art of expressing God in such a way that everything in this nature knows who, how and what truly God is, then we have entered the true realm of life. This is simply to mean that, what gives life a true meaning is the ability to express God if possible in His fullness. It will be truly impossible to express God without knowing how He is and His ways of doing things. Nevertheless, there's still a way of truly knowing God and have proof that we know Him.

By the grace of the progressive revelation and understanding of God; this book will be helping us on how we can truly know God and have proof to our generation that we know Him.

Checking on the creation and introduction of mankind into this planet, you will notice that the greatest vision of God about mankind was for mankind to look like Him (*Genesis 1:26* "*... let us make man in our image...*" *kjv*). Meaning all these other things came secondary, even us having authority and dominion was something to happen after we already look like Him.

So the assignment of mankind is to look like God and express Him to all creation, meaning we were to govern or rule as gods on behalf of God such that when the creation likes at us it sees God. Until we master the ability to express God to all the creation, it's only a lie to say that we are in His will.

When you continue checking the scripture quoted above, you will notice that it then talks about mankind having dominion over everything on earth (*"... let them have dominion over all the earth and over everything upon the earth". kjv*) This was and still the mind of God about mankind especially to them who are called by His name, the ones who are born not of the will of man but of God and these are the true believers, the sons of the Most High God.

It was never in God's plan for mankind to be dominated here on earth as it is in our days. Not even the devil, nor his demons were to dominate over mankind as men are now submitting to spirits. We were never supposed to fear anything, because when you fear anything you only proving insecurity of authority over the thing you fear.

It's true we were created to exercise dominion and rule this earth on behalf of God, but then what happened, why is it that we keep on failing even when we claim to be on the right track?

No matter how much we can call ourselves children of God, the truth remains that we continue misrepresenting God by our inability to express Him to this earth in His fullness. This is the same reason why the testimony of our being born again is not shown at all. Remember according to Jesus, those who believe must be able to cast out devils, speak in new tongues and even to lay hands on the sick to recover.

Mark 16:17-18 "and these signs shall follow them that believe; In my name shall they cast out devils; they shall speak with new tongues; they shall take up serpents; and if they drink any deadly thing, it shall not hurt them; they shall lay hands on the sick and they shall recover." KJV

Will it be wrong for me to say these sings are the ones to determine whether one is a true believer or not? I know this is crazy because most of those who believe don't really experience these signs. If Jesus means exactly what He's saying, then we have a serious problem as the family of believers. Notice that Jesus never said the signs shall follow pastors or preachers, but whosoever believes. I can attest on the fact that what Jesus is saying is only possible if we are in the very same God's plan, He had from the beginning.

"What really happened to the church, why are we not able to experience what is expected of us as sons of God? "

Because of our failure to express God in His true nature; we turned to develop different theologies and doctrines around our limitations which then created different denominations about the very same God we serve. And this has tempered with our belief system and made us to be comfortable regardless of us not experiencing what we should be experiencing as believers.

Have you ever asked yourself the question of "why are we having so many churches with many different believes yet under the same umbrella of Christianity?"; to me this only proves that there is much of man's doctrine than Gods doctrine in our churches. This is honestly because; it doesn't make any sense to believe in the same God who gave us the same vision yet have so many disagreements about the same God we believe in.

For example; why some churches believe in the speaking of tongues and some don't, yet we all claim to come from the same source.

This is honestly not to castigate the body of Christ, but it a calling unto deep. There is more in God than what we have settled for. There is a greater understand of God that God is inviting us to, a level of accuracy and assurance of the things which are in God. A dimension of proof for the things of God with a life experience, such that the spiritual realities are not only true as revealed by bible history but can be a reality in our life experience. We can believe the things of God not only because they have been captured in history but because we have experienced them in our life time.

The more I studied the scriptures, is the more I realized how far we are from what we say we are. What we call "church" in our days is a lot different from what was the church as revealed by bible history. What we call a "Christian" today is a lot different than what a Christian is as revealed by scriptures. The disciples of Jesus Christ our Lord were first called Christians in Antioch (*see Acts 11:26*) because they looked and behaved like Christ.

Looking at the church today, checking on our behavior and the way we present ourselves; is it really the way Christ is? If we are to earn the name of being called Christians by looking and behaving like Christ, sometimes I really feel like it's an insult to Jesus Christ to call ourselves "Christians".

I'm not trying to make the Christian life hard, but only trying to fill up the gapes in our journey of Christianity and faith such that we don't full ourselves into thinking that we have done well yet we didn't. We can get to that accuracy just like the apostle Paul when he said "I have fought a good fight, I have finished my course, I have kept the faith and I can even see the reward of my good labor" (*see 2Timothy 4:7-8*). There are those who are going to be caught by surprise on the day of the Lord, who thought they have done well only to find on the last moments that they never really did well to enter into the Kingdom of Heaven (*see Matthew 7:21-23*). They really thought they have done well but when the lexicon of the spirit is check they were found unworthy of the Kingdom of God. I truly don't want to be part of that team and this is the reason why we should get to the level of accuracy about our relationship with God, and this book is to open our eyes unto how can that be possible.

In God's plan; the church was supposed to be a representative government of God here on earth to legislate and execute the Will of God on earth as it is in heaven, yet when you look at things now; the church is only considered to be a religious institution. This simply means that the church was supposed to be the most powerful organization on earth but the current reality is that the church is the weakest organization governed by individuals who have no respect of what we believe in.

When you look back in history, you will notice that the church was trusted to have solutions of national problems while the current church is the last to be considered to have solutions of our national problems.

The church is now more like an option for losers because we have failed as the church to represent heaven in it true nature. Man must rise who will stand for the Kingdom we represent in truth and in power to this evil generation which has made God to be a cheap commodity, yet God is far above and priceless. The church was a house of wealth yet today it is believed to be wrong for the church to have more wealth.

That is why the church is having less if not non wealth (*see Malachi 3:10*), yet the church was supposed to be controlling and managing wealth. There is a way we can reclaim our position of authority as the church and truly reveal God in His true nature and this book is leading us toward that direction.

There are many spiritual realities we can't even talk about in this generation because we have failed to justify them through our life experience. We can't even stand boldly in supporting those spiritual realities because we don't even know whether they are truly true or are just stories created to make men believe.

This is an invitation into a place where we can believe on these spiritual realities not only because they have been captured in history but because they are a reality in our lives. It's time we teach doctrines that can be proven through our life experience, not just by scripture but through life reality. Remember Jesus never only taught but He also demonstrated what He was teaching (*Acts 1:1* "*... of all that Jesus began both to do and teach, kjv*).

We can notice that Jesus did not only teach but He also proved in action what he was teaching. There is a great secret about the ministry of Jesus Christ that we are going to reveal shortly.

Away with this mentality of just teaching only and believing that things will change, no! We must come to a level whereby we can prove with action what we teach and let it be evidence in our lifetime. If we say the devil have no power and all power is of God given to the church, then someone must come and prove that. It can't remain true as revealed by bible history. Just like those we read about from the scriptures; let us also have evidence of our experience with God, to prove to our generation that God is real.

Living a resurrected life can help us to restore our dignity as the church and experience God with proof to our generation that God is with us!

Chapter one

Believers Retreat

As the church of God; we have the responsibility to look and behave like God, we have the responsibility to bring and execute the Will of God here on earth as it is in Heaven and we can never accomplish these responsibilities unless God help us.

We have strived up to this far and achieved all we have achieved, but still we are not reaching to the perfection of God. We have learned, studied, meditated and believed on the spiritual realities about God, yet still there are realities that has never been a reality in experience to the current church.

It is true; there are voices in the church that are now louder than the Voice of God itself. There are men in the church that are now more honored and respected than God Himself. Pride has grown in the church to a level whereby we can't even see it, because it has become our normal daily experience. We have honestly shifted from our rightful position as the church. Again this is not to make us feel bad or weak as the church, but a restoration of the true principles of God to the church.

It's high-time we retreat to a more favorable position and start crying for backup. It high time we withdraw from our pride and go back to the original plan of God. If there is something we have lost somewhere as the church, it's time we revisit the drawing book and check our foundations such that we can reclaim our position of being the government of God here on earth to execute the original plan of God about the church.

When I'm talking about the church I'm not really talking about those born of bible exegesis but those who are born of the spirit, because many have been convicted into becoming the church just by the study of scriptures yet the church is far more than just studying scriptures.

Let's not forget that scriptures carry men experience with God and how God revealed Himself to them. If we are to only know God through other men's experience with Him, then we have no knowledge of that God.

If it true that God has called us into a personal relationship with Him; how is it then personal if it's always going to be valued by someone else experience? We need that personal experience with God so that we can explain Him to our generation the way He has revealed Himself to us. I know there is a believe out there which says "every natural experience proofs that God is with us", yes; to some extend this is true, but let's never forget that the God we talking about is "supernatural". Meaning there is the dimension of God that is supernatural and we still have to experience that.

Honestly, to me it's dangerous to only know God through scriptures with no personal experience if it's true that He is our loving Father. After all; the scriptures were written so that man will believe that Jesus is the Christ (*see John 20:31*) and also profitable for doctrine (*see 2 Timothy 3:16-17*), but all this doesn't mean we shouldn't have an experience with God.

I am not saying we would come up with our own scripture as by how God has revealed Himself to us, but we can believe and have sound doctrine through the scriptures and when it comes to demonstrating God; we can do that as a result of our encounter with Him.

So let us never forget that revelation is progressive from generation to generation. This is to mean that, there can be a way God would love to reveal Himself with, which has never been captured in history. Let's not limit Him to His historical revelations when there can be more.

The partials of old who walked the journey of faith with God, have overcame and achieved a lot by their faith and now they stand as a great cloud of witnesses only to prove the possibilities of faith and the faithfulness of God to those who truly believes in Him. (*Hebrews 12:1 "wherefore seeing we also are compassed about with so great a cloud of witnesses ." kjv*).

They walked the journey of faith and they did overcome just to show me and you that we can overcome if we can grab some few lessons from them. They now carry a great testimony of their faith and experience with God which is what is lacking to the current church. When you check on their testimony, its more about their experience with God and how God revealed Himself to them and all the achievements they had as a result of their relationship with God.

This mostly is what is lacking to the current church. We have less in testimony of our journey with God, and most of what we call our testimonies of faith are things even the world (meaning people who are not of the family of faith) can and have achieved. These are just things we achieve by the grace and mercy of God or even just following the principles of life. Yet there are those things that must come to us as a result of our faith and relationship with God. Things which people that are not of faith cannot have.

It is important that we understand that in the economy of the spirit or in the dealings of God with man, not everything is a gift. There are those things which are gifts, but there are also those which come as a reward of understanding and keeping the principles of faith.

For example: in the book of *Mark 9:41* Jesus said "*whosoever shall give you a cup of water to drink in my name, because you belong to Christ, shall not lose his reward.*" *kjv*

You can notice that Jesus is talking about someone not losing something as a result of him keep a principle of giving something to those who belong to Christ. This means you can secure a blessing over your life just by observing a principle and likewise the next person who did not observe the principle will not have that same blessing, which then makes that blessing to be a reward and not a gift.

So there are those things that we must achieve as a result of our faith and experience with God. This is what we call the testimony of faith; just like what James talked about when he was teaching on faith, (*James 2:17* "*even so faith, if it hath not works, is dead, being it alone.*" *kjv*) And this simply means there is no faith if there are no works to prove your faith. Let's have something tangible to prove and support our faith because faith alone is dead.

At individual level we must have works and achievements as a result of our faith to justify our experience with God and the reason why we believe. According to apostle Peter; as we continue in the journey of faith we must be always ready to give a reason of our belief and hope (*see 1Peter 3:15*), meaning there has to be a way to justify your relationship with God. So we need those things which are beyond humanity to justify to the world that we represent a kingdom far above this world and this may be a great chance to restore our dignity as the church.

As I have highlighted earlier; there are signs that should follow those who believe, and by these signs we should be able to justify our belief and level of faith. If the church does not experience these signs, then it's time we go back and check what went wrong or question ourselves the very question many don't like "are we really true believers?". This might be the way to believers retreat.

This is not church politics but a calling unto an accountability of knowing God with prove that we know Him. It's a calling unto a true fellowship with God such that we do not only know about Him but get to know Him, because there is a difference between knowing God and knowing about God. The more we study scriptures is the more we get to know about God yet knowing Him will require one to be in true fellowship with Him. Just like what Jesus said about people rushing to scriptures and rejecting Him in person.

===

John 5:39-40 "search the scriptures; for in them ye think ye have eternal life: and they are they which testify of me. And ye will not come to me, that ye might have life". kjv

This is one scripture that scholars of the bible don't want us to check in details because it reveals something wrong that we keep on doing on daily basis and yet have it justified to be the right thing to do,

First and foremost; Jesus is revealing that there is a significant difference between Him and the scriptures and eternal life is not with the scriptures but with Him. Jesus made it clear that the scriptures, they only attest of Him meaning they carry information about Him. Some translations like NLT put it like "the scripture is a hand pointing unto me" meaning they are not me but they can lead you to me.

It's more like seeing a board written Johannesburg is 21km west then you rest saying you in Johannesburg, no; that would be a wrong address because you still to travel 21km more.

The people that Jesus was addressing were rejecting Him in person and choosing to rest in the scriptures yet the scriptures are only a hand pointing to Him and they don't have the life but it is Him(Jesus) who carries the life. And in the name of honestly, this is the same problem we have even up to today. We have rested on the scriptures thinking that we are in Christ yet we are just on a board pointing unto Him.

This may be as a result of our theological background which taught us that the scriptures are the word of God yet Jesus Christ is the Word of God (*Revelations 19:13 "and he was clothed with a vesture dipped in blood: and his name is called The Word of God." kjv*)

We will need more than just scriptures to truly know God, scriptures are given by inspiration profitable for sound doctrine (*see 2 Timothy 3:16*), but they shouldn't stop us from a true fellowship with God. Sometimes we do reject God unaware through the knowledge we have of Him and limit His operations in and through our lives.

Our success as the church is hidden in keeping His patterns and being in true fellowship with Him not just information about Him because many are in fellowship with information about Him and not Him in person.

I'm not saying people should stop their fellowship with the scriptures, but I'm just saying let them be known of what they truly are and let them not replace the true fellowship we should have with God. Meditating on the scriptures is basic and very important in our journey with God, but it's very important to accept them of what they truly are.

And again; let us not forget that scriptures as they are given by the inspiration of the Holy Spirit, they need the Holy Spirit for proper interpretation and understanding. Meaning more than just having the scriptures to read we need the Holy Spirit that will lead us into proper understanding just like as Jesus said that the spirit will lead us to all the truth.

Let it be known that proper interpretation and understanding of scripture is more important than the scripture itself.

The giants of faith, the partials of old who successfully walked the journey of faith and stand as witness; the bible is not ashamed to give us their testimony and good works of faith (*see Hebrews 11:32*). To my amazement, they obtained a good report not having the promise (Holy Spirit) of God which we now have (*see Hebrews 11:39*) yet when you closely look at their report, you will notice that their work appears to be better than ours yet again they didn't have the holy spirit as we do now. By the look of things, we should be having a better report because we now have a quickening spirit to enable us to do the business of faith more that the ordinal humans faith.

Even Jesus after He has taught His disciples about three years He still insisted that they remain in Jerusalem until they are empowered for the business of faith (*see Luke 24:49*). This means that even Jesus understood that the business of faith does not just need your theological background but power if we are to succeed and this power is coming only through attaining a life from above.

And the disciples of Jesus remained in Jerusalem and never went to do the work of faith unless and until they were empowered for that kind of business. As a result of their waiting, the promise of the Father came and empowered them to go and do the work of ministry, and this is one reason why they succeeded in the things of God for God was with them.

In our days, many are just preaching and teaching just because they did well at their different schools of ministry and not really considered to be spiritually empowered for that kind of work. This is the reason the church is growing weaker; we keep on preaching and not being able to demonstrate what we are teaching because we were never really spiritually empowered for that kind of business.

It's very important to see that you are empowered for what you wake up to do each day, especially in the things of God.

The bible then goes on to declare that by the hands of the apostles; many signs and wonders were done because they were now empowered for that kind of business (*see Acts 2:43, Acts 4:30, Acts 5:12, Acts 14:3*).

I believe there is a great movement in the things of the spirit. And God is inviting us to a place of accuracy in the things of the spirit. Whereby the things we read about from scriptures can be a reality in our lives and we can move with God not according to history but according to what God is up to do as of the now happenings.

Our retreat will be helping us to draw closer to the mind of God about us as the current church and guarantee our victory which we have in Christ Jesus. We shall truly rise to the room of authority as the current church and rule from a place where it is impossible to fail. There is a life we can live whereby we have assurance that everything we do is exactly what God wants and expect from us.

====

We salute the great Gods generals of old; the likeness of Roberts Liardon, Smith Wigglesworth, Maria Woodworth Etter, Benson Idahose, Reinhard Bonnke, Kathryn Kuhlman and many other partials of old who took it to themselves to spread the gospel of Jesus with power, held great revivals of fire and brought souls to Christ in the records of history. They were many other great movements which never got the chance to be captured in history. These are men and women of God who are long gone to be with God yet because of their walk with God; their stories are being told up to today.

For the likeness of Reinhard Bonnke who did spread the gospel of Christ with power across the world mostly in Africa. He brought the foundations of faith to many, calling great revivals of fire which brought millions to Christ and in the history of captured revivals in Africa He still stand as one who held the greatest.

We really salute and honor them for their great work and we thank God for those movements which were captured for us to have evidence that the move of God never ended with those we read about from scripture. They really did the best they could with the grace and revelation which was available for them during their time. They explained the mysteries of God the best way they understood them and they revealed God the way they knew Him. If it wasn't of their sacrifices maybe some of us we wouldn't have known the true gospel of Jesus Christ with power. I believe they are at rest with the Father being rewarded for their great walk of faith with God.

Knowing that revelation is progressive and in the lexicon of the spirit; latter glory is expected to be greater than the former (*see Haggai 2:9*), we must know that the things that God is to do with our generation are greater than anything we have seen or heard in history. So let us not limit God into past experiences when God is calling us into greater dimensions.

We can attest to the fact that the world is growing more evil and wicked with time yet this should also be a wakeup call to the church to advance in power. Now I know the devil improves every after each battle and this is why we must also improve in strength and power as the church because whether we like it or not; we are in a spiritual war fare which we are expected to win.

As from the days of the apostles of Jesus Christ, the gospel of the kingdom has been preached as Jesus instructed them to go and preach the gospel of the kingdom (*see Matthew 24:14*). Even Jesus Himself, He went about preaching not just any gospel but the gospel of the kingdom (*see Matthew 4:23*). Have you ever thought of why Jesus was so specific about the preaching of the gospel of the kingdom?

For years I have tried to bring my theological education in trying to real understand what the gospel of the kingdom is and why Jesus insisted on the preaching of the gospel for the kingdom. Come to think of it; do we even know what the gospel of the kingdom real is? I suppose this is where many have lost it and this makes our foundations of faith to be questionable.

Firstly, we must understand that we are a generation of the new covenant of God which is through Christ Jesus meaning the resurrected Jesus, (because there is a different between Jesus and Christ Jesus which will be explained in details as we continue). But in short we can say Jesus Christ is the phrase of Jesus who is born of Marry (the Jesus of Nazareth) and Christ Jesus is the phrase of Jesus after the cross (meaning the resurrected Jesus). I hope you have noticed that from the book of Acts in the bible Jesus is then referred to as Christ Jesus not Jesus Christ and that was for a very significant reason.

We are the generation of the new covenant, meaning there is the old covenant which God did with the children of Israel through Abraham down to Moses and this covenant has really nothing much to do with us especially we as gentiles. In due time God then brought the new covenant which will then cover everyone as long as they believe in His son Jesus Christ.

It clearly doesn't make sense to bring a new covenant if the old is still working perfectly fine. This simple mean there is a problem with the old covenant and that's why God had to bring up the superior and final covenant to cover the shame of the old (*see Hebrews 8:13*). It's amazing how we still have people holding on to the old covenant when it's actually decaying and vanishing away; they will vanish with it.

Let it be clearly known; we are not under the covenant of the laws of Moses, but under the covenant of the love of God through the blood of Jesus Christ. And this is the foundation of our faith; we have faith because Jesus is the author and the finisher of our faith (*see Hebrews 12:2*).

And this brings us to the fact that there is only one gospel to be preached and that is the "Gospel of

Jesus Christ". The gospel of Jesus Christ is simple the Love of God demonstrated to the world (*see John 3:16*), for God so loved the world and as a result He sacrificed His only son for the world to have life. The gospel of Jesus Christ is an umbrella with two sub headings under it; the Gospel of Salvation and the Gospel of the Kingdom which brings all the rewards and benefits of being in the new covenant. These two do have their differences; firstly, the gospel of salvation has much to do with what God has done for us while the gospel of the kingdom has everything to do with our response to what God has done for us.

So in preaching the gospel of Jesus Christ we touch on what God has done for us which is the gospel of salvation and is just once and for all. Then we stick deeper about what is expected of us as a result of what God has done for us and this is the gospel of the kingdom. You can then notice that; repentance, wellness, holiness and even worship fall under the gospel of the kingdom because it is more about what we are to do as a result of what God has done for us.

The apostle Paul once indicated that there is a chance that one can be always learning but never come to the knowledge of truth (*see 2 Timothy 3:7*), and honestly I find this to be very true and practical. The way we have structured our teaching and learning programs in our different churches is the most likely reason why many never reach to the knowledge of truth.

In preaching the gospel we must only preach the gospel of Christ and in administering the gospel of Christ, we must also understand that we first have to introduce the gospel of salvation for bringing people into the kingdom of God. But when people are now in the kingdom; we are supposed to teach the gospel of the Kingdom, so that people will then understand and know their responsibilities in the kingdom.

If we are to truly reach into perfection as the church, we must understand that we must know what God has done for us together with our response and duties from what God has done for us.

So the relationship of God with mankind is not centered on what God is to do for us, but also what we are to do for Him and this is what we call "true fellowship with God". It's clear now that Jesus insisted on the gospel of the kingdom because God's part has been done perfectly well, what is left is our response to what has already been made available for us. The message of salvation is very important, but let's never think it is more important than the message of the kingdom.

Personally I believe that since the message of the kingdom has much to do with our response to what God has done for us; it is the message to be preached more if we are to establish a successful true church and building the members of the body of Christ.

As for the gospel being preached; it must the loud and clear that there is only one gospel to be preached which is the gospel of Jesus Christ because it is the gospel we preach that determines whether we know God or not. And John puts it this way;

2 John 1:9-11 "Whosoever transgresseth, and abideth not in the doctrine of Christ, hath not God. He that abideth in the doctrine of Christ, he hath both the Father and the Son. If there come any unto you, and bring not this doctrine, receive him not into your house, neither bid him God speed: for he that biddeth him God speed is partaker of his evil deeds". kjv

This is one less used scripture in preaching because it challenges our relationship with God through the doctrine we teach. The writer makes it clear that the doctrine you preach determines if you truly know God or not and it is in the gospel of Christ where one can only be with both God and the Son. It's only when we abide in the doctrine of Christ that we can be sure that we have God and the Son because any other doctrine only proves that we have no fellowship with the Father and the Son. If someone comes to you with any other doctrine which is not the doctrine of Christ; the bible makes it clear that you are never supposed to receive that person, don't even greet him because by greeting him you a partaking to his evil deeds.

How serious is this? I know many like to preach and teach from the Old Testament scriptures and this might be because they have no revelation of the Christ in their lives. But the fact still remains if anything you choose to focus on do not reveal the Christ then you must know you don't have God and the Son in you. It may be a teaching from Moses or any of the prophets of old; if it doesn't reveal the Christ, God is not there because it's only Christ who connects us to the Father in the new covenant. This may sound disrespectful but it is the truth. Knowledge about Jesus is not enough without the revelation of the Christ because the revelation about the Christ is what makes us to be sons of God.

Remember a child was born but the son was given (*see Isaiah 9:6*), the child born is Jesus who was born of Marry but the son given is the Christ who was given by the Father and it is in the Son(Christ) that we get to be sons of God not with the child. So if it's only Jesus there is no qualification of the son, because being a son of God is not with Jesus but with the revelation of the Christ. So let it be known that we are only to dwell with the doctrine of Christ if we are to truly perfect the Will of God.

As time hit by; our educational systems in the things of the spirit motivated us to over focus on the rewards of being in the new covenant than the gospel itself. Just like how the message of going to heaven is over preached. It has been preached in such a way that everyone is motivated to work as hard as possible just to go to heaven yet it was never really Gods plan for us to go to heaven. It's just something that came as a result of failure to accomplish the primal mandate of God about mankind. We were supposed to make earth heaven by bringing the culture of heaven here on earth as it is in heaven. And this is what Jesus told His disciples when He was teaching them how to pray;

(Matthew 6:10 "Thy kingdom come. Thy will be done in earth, as it is in heaven." kjv).

We over preach on the things which God can do for us if we come to him, and that's the reason why now people come to God because of what He can do yet we were never supposed to come to God because of what He can do for us, but we are to come to Him because of who He Is. Let there be a balance in the preaching of the gospel!

Let us stop this mentality of using God for our own pride and success, God is not that stupid. God is rising a generation of true worshipers, who will worship Him despite of what He can do for them. A Generation of believers who their only desire will be to look more like God. God is rising a generation of believers who will stay in His presence and know what is to be in the presence of God. God is calling us into a place where we can achieve things that can't be bought with money.

I once heard one great speaker some year back saying "if all you have can be bought with money then you don't have much". I started to think about the things we desire in life and I noticed most of them can be bought with money and that means they are manmade. Most of manmade products no matter how valuable they are, you can still find a fake version of it yet there are those things which are heavenly supplied and you don't see a fake version of it. We shall reveal some as we continue as the spirit leads us.

Our educational systems have discouraged us from experiencing God by reducing our experiences of God to what only can be proven scriptural. Like, if your experience has never been captured scriptural then it's not considered to be of God. So now we turn to expect God to reveal Himself the way He did in history. In our days' things which can't be proven scriptural are not considered to be Godly yet in the very same scriptures; the experiences of some of those we read about were thing that never existed in history.

For example; the woman with the issue of blood for twelve years in the book of *Luke 8:43-48*, after she heard that Jesus was to cross around she made up her mind to go just only to touch the border of Jesus' garment and her issue was solved. The point is that she heard an experience that never existed before now we talking about it because she decided to do something that was never done before.

Actually the scripture itself admits that not everything was recorded (*see John 20:30-31*), but still we want to prove everything by what is written knowing very well that some things are not written. There is more in God that what we know from history because He's not only the God of the past but also the God of the now and the future (*see Hebrews 13:8*). Let us not limit God to past experiences but allow Him to be who He is. There are higher dimensions of God than what has been captured in history and we stand a chance to experience them in our generation. They limited God in history (*Psalms 78:41*) why repeat the same problem when we have a chance to do better.

Most of those we read about from the scriptures never really had the bible to value their relationship with God using, but they explained God and even wrote the scriptures after their personal experience with God. I'm not saying we should be writing scriptures, no; but what I'm trying to say is that if we will limit and value our relationship with God through someone else experience with God, then how are we even sure that we know Him?

There was a time when Jesus said if we believe in Him we can do what He has done and even more as a result of Him going to the Father (*see John 14:12*). The scholars of the bible are still having a problem with this particular scripture because of the reasoning behind "what can be more than what Jesus has done" yet Jesus was talking about all the works of faith that He was doing.

If we are truly to do all the works of Jesus and even more; how are we supposed to know that which was not recorded if we are only focusing on that which was recorded? This scripture also reveals to us that is not everything Jesus demonstrated, there still more in God which Jesus is expecting us to do as a result of Him being with the Father. But then again; how are we supposed to know the thing we are to do as a result of Him being in heaven, because that means those things are not yet revealed to humankind.

All these are the reasons why God is inviting us into a Life that is Greater where all these things are possible.

In as much as nothing is impossible with God; Jesus opened our eyes to the fact that we can also experience that same ability only if we can have faith and in His description faith as a grain of a mustard seed (*see Matthew 17:20*). I have noticed that most of what we quote and believe from scriptures we don't really give ourselves times to check it in detail for deeper understanding. What was Jesus really talking about here? Because he even said you can instruct a mountain and it can listen. If the subject it's just faith; how come, we do have faith yet in reality there is a lot of things which remains impossible in our lives.

Many then choose to attach the size of faith when trying to explain this scripture, but then again what are you talking about when you speak of the size of faith? I have noticed that in most times we turn to explain scripture without considering the altitude where the scripture is spoken from and we interpret it from our level only for it to make sense to us at our level, yet that sometimes alters the message and we can end up receiving a wrong message or not receiving any message at all.

Just like when a voice came from heaven in the book of *John 12:28-30*; Jesus prayed to God and His message was "Father, glorify thy name" and as a result a voice came from heaven saying "I have both glorified it, and will glorify it again". The people who were there with Jesus also heard the voice but they gave it a different interpretation because they never heard it from where it was spoken from. Some said it was thundering and some said it an angel speaking to Jesus, yet according to Jesus the message was clear "I have both glorified it, and I will glorify it again".

And when Jesus responded to them, He made it clear that the message came because of them yet still they were not able to correctly perceive the message. This is honestly the reason why many of these scriptures remain a mystery in as much as we claim to understand them.

There are messages sent from a phone with a higher operating system which will not make sense if are received by a phone with a lower operating system, and this is why it's very important to attain that ability to be in the same altitude from where the message is sent or spoken if you are to get the correct message. And there is a provision for that through the principle of living a resurrected life.

Chapter two

WHAT IS THIS RESURRECTED LIFE?

Romans 6:4 "Therefore we are buried with him by baptism into death: that like as Christ was raised up from the dead by the glory of the Father, even so we should walk in newness of life. "kjv

There is a life that I will call the Greater Life, a life that is superior to the life we experience and this is the life which makes up for the possibilities of the things of the spirit. This is the life which was predestined for us as sons of God long before the creation of mankind. It is the life that was in the mind of God for/about mankind long before the introduction of sin and the fall of man. It is in this life where we as mankind have authority above everything in this world including every spirit that will find itself in this world. And we rule above all while we are only ruled by God the creator of the universe.

The Greater Life is a life we live whereby sin and death have no power over us since we carry the nature of God which can never be corrupted by sin and death. It is only in this greater life can we truly represent God in His true nature and still live as human being just like how Jesus did during the days of his flesh.

In this greater life there is no fear, sorrow or pain but only peace and joy where you need not to worry about anything because you know everything is under your control. I know; because of the reality of this distorted life we live in, many thinks of this greater life as impossible, yet if we can remember Jesus said there is a life we can live where nothing is impossible not just only to God but also to us (*see Matthew 17:20*).

How great it is to wake up each day knowing that everything is under your authority? The greater life is the best way to describe the love of God for mankind.

Because of the introduction of sin and the fall of man, we lost our position in living this greater life. We lost the authority given to us by the Father and started to submit to spirits which were supposed to be submitting to us for as long as they are here on earth. God being a loving and kind God never let go of His primal plan about mankind of having authority over all the earth and everything in it. He came up with a great plan of restoring this greater life to mankind such that we can still execute His plan of having to rule earth on His behalf.

This plan is what is called the Resurrected Life, whereby we die from our old life and resurrect into the greater life through the principle of the death and resurrection of Jesus Christ. As a result of the principle of death and resurrection; the greater life is now called the resurrected life or the newness of life which is actually the same life we were to life before the introduction of sin and the fall of man.

===

Each and every year; we as Christians celebrate the death and the resurrection of Jesus Christ as a very remarkable event in the history of Christianity. Honestly there are many different interpretations behind the death and the resurrection of Jesus Christ depending on our different levels of understanding the spiritual life. But one most important thing we must understand about the death and the resurrection of Jesus Christ is that His death was of a different purpose than His resurrection. Meaning the benefits of His death are different from the benefits of His resurrection. He died to separate us from our sinful life, but that's not the same reason why He resurrected.

Many do understand the death of Jesus Christ, but when it comes to His resurrection; there are deeper mysteries behind His resurrection which we are still to reveal and understand. As for His death; we know that He died to take anyway our sins but we never really give ourselves time to understand on how is that happening.

Remember the kingdom of God is governed by what is called the Kingdom Principles of God and one of them is the Principle of Seed Faith. Generally; when a seed is planting it's because it has to give birth to more of its kind yet that's not the only thing happening when a seed is planted. It is believed that when a seed is planted for a moment it experiences death before it can geminate into becoming a new plant. So the seed dies from its old nature and life so that it can resurrect into a new life and nature.

So in the principle of Seed Faith; everything that is tied to the nature of that seed is expected to die as the seed dies from its old nature such that when it resurrects, all those things which were tied to that seed are expected to have died as the seed died before resurrecting into a new life.

This is to mean that in the economy of the spirit, sometimes we plant seeds not because we want to reap more of its kind but because we want to kill certain things tied on the seed we plant. And this is exactly how the remuneration of our sins happened. Our sins were tied to Jesus as he was nailed on the cross and as He dies they died to, such that when He resurrects they are no more there.

Notice it's not only our sins which were tied on Jesus as He died on the cross but also our old lives such that as he dies my old life dies with Him and in His resurrection we are resurrected together with Him into a new life, and this is done through the principle of baptism. So baptism to us now does not symbolizes repentance as the baptism of John (*see Acts 19:4*) but it symbolizes our death with Christ and our resurrection into the new life, just as Paul said in the scripture quoted above.

Jesus died for the remission of our sins and He resurrected for us to attain a new life and that is the Resurrected Life. The life we live after resurrection not a physical resurrection but a resurrection by the principle of baptism and the death of Jesus.

There is something that must happen during baptism which unlock this new life just like what happened with Jesus when He was baptized by John in river Jordan (*see Matthew 3:16*), but this will be discussed in details later when we talk about being born again. So a Resurrected Life is the life we live after we have received something from heaven as a result of resurrecting with Jesus.

Having your sins forgiven doesn't mean you then automatically receive the resurrected life, because the resurrected life is not with the death of Jesus Christ but with the resurrection with him. Which means you can have your sins forgiven and be a believer but not yet living a resurrected life and this is why we are all invited into this life.

When Paul was writing to the saints in Philippi, he put it in a way which reveals that you can be a believer but not yet unto the perfection of living this resurrected life (*see Philippians 3:7-16*). He first put us into a position of seeing the prize of knowing Christ, he said he is ready to loss everything which is of gain to Him only for the excellency of the knowledge of Christ Jesus. If the man is willing to loss everything just only to know Christ, you can just imagine what is it to truly know Christ. And then he also said he wants to know the power of His resurrection, meaning as far as for that time when he wrote to them, Paul was still to know certain mysteries behind the resurrection of Jesus Christ. Furthermore, he also indicates that he wants to participate in this resurrected life meaning he is not yet there but working towards there.

While he still working toward attaining that life, he highlighted things he is doing like forgetting the past and focusing on the things ahead and this is because the past can distract us from attaining the resurrected life. But finally he revealed that if we have already attained this life then let walk by the same rule, and this then proves to us that we can attain this life which is greater than what we have experienced before or what we are experiencing currently.

In the likeness of the death and resurrection of Jesus Christ, we attain the same spirit that rose up Christ from the dead and that spirit it then quickens our mortal bodies (*see Romans 8:11*) such that as Christ was raised from the dead we are also raised into this resurrected life.

Just like how Paul put it in *Romans 6:4*, that as a result of the resurrection of Christ and having the same spirit that raised Jesus from the death; there is an expectation by heaven from us to live in the newness of life. Meaning if it's true that we have the same spirit that raised Jesus form the dead, heaven is expecting us to live the resurrected life because in the economy of God, that spirit must give us the ability to live a superior life than the life we had before.

The resurrected life is the system which gives us power over the kingdom of darkness and its principalities. It helps us to execute the Will of God of bringing the culture of Heaven here on earth as it is in Heaven, and this is the true meaning of the phrase "Heaven on Earth". This resurrected life helps us to host the same presence of God here on earth as it is in heaven, such that there is no difference whether God is in Heaven or on earth.

In greater terms; the resurrected life is the life we live from Heaven. Oh yes it is true; there is a life we can live from heaven. Through the same principle of the resurrection of Jesus Christ and our baptism with water and the spirit of God, we are raised together with Christ and made to sit together with Him in the heavenly places far above all principalities, power, might and dominion

(see Ephesians1:20-23 and Ephesians 2:5-6).

When you can notice; Paul used past tense in his writing to make it clear that he is not talking about a life after a physical death, but he is talking about an experience as a result of the death and resurrection of Jesus Christ. Meaning by this resurrected life we are already seated in the heavenly places with Christ Jesus. If we are to live any life, then we live it from where we are seated in the heavenly places with Christ Jesus.

Colossians 3:3 "for ye are dead and your life is hid with Christ in God" kjv

You can notice that in this scripture, the apostle Paul is making it clear that your life is not with you but hidden in Christ who is in God in Heaven. In verse four; Paul then said this Christ is our life, and this makes us to have no life of our own but the life of Christ such that it's no longer me who lives but the Christ in me.

Just like what Paul said in *Galatians 2:20* *"I am crucified with Christ: nevertheless I live; yet not I, but Christ liveth in me: and the life which I now live in the flesh I live it by the faith of the Son of God, who loved me, and gave himself for me.kjv.*

In this scripture; we understand that on the basis of Paul being crucified with Christ, it's no longer him who lives but the Christ yet there is still a life he is living in the flesh. Knowing that Christ is seated in the right hand of the Father and our lives are in Him; the only way to live that life is to live it from where Christ is seated.

All this is only to prove that we can live our life from a world far from this. In this resurrected life we are called to live a heavenly life here on earth and Jesus is a perfect example to us because during His days on earth, He lived a heavenly life while on earth breading earthly air. Some choose to call this "living a dual life", meaning a spirit life and a physical life at the same time. But for me it's just one life "the Spirit Life" in different forms depending on your whereabouts.

In heaven it's a spirit life in a spiritual body and on earth it's still a spirit life in a physical body. If we can study the life of Jesus while He was here on earth, we'll notice that He lived a spirit life which helped Him to succeed in executing His mission on earth as it was expected of Him. And this makes him a perfect example we can look up to on how to live a spirit life while here on earth.

The way Jesus came here on earth was a picture of how we are also to come here on earth and live a heavenly life just as He did. I know this might be confusing, but it will make perfect sense as we continue because we still have to touch deeper on what it really means to receive Jesus Christ. Some of these things we think we know them yet they have never been revealed in details for better understanding, because receiving Jesus is not just about the confession by mouth and believing that Jesus is lord, then surrendering all your old ways to adopt the ways of Jesus; there's truly more than that.

===

Many like to think that the success of Jesus Christ in His mission was as a result of Him being the perfect son of God and somehow his supernaturally coming from heaven; yet He was human just like me and you only strengthened and equipped by this spirit life the same way we should also be quickened. Remember Jesus was the firstborn of many other sons to come (*see Romans 8:29*), logically it makes no sense to call your child a firstborn if he/she is the only child.

So Jesus is the firstborn because there are many other sons including me and you. The creation has been waiting for the manifestation of the sons of God (*see Romans 8:19*), and by the time Paul wrote this, Jesus was already manifested, so it can't be Jesus that the creation is waiting for; but other sons including me and you.

So away with this mentality of thinking that Jesus succeeded in His mission because He was a miraculous child of God. The actual truth is that, He was a picture of how we should be as sons of God, and as long as we see His success as a result of Him being a miracle child, we will never be truly conformed to His image and overcome as He did. Jesus Christ is our super-hero not only for us to praise him but also to learn from Him and follow His footsteps. We are not just His followers but His disciples, meaning we are to learn from Him more than just following Him and His work.

Actually the idea of us being called Christians was never really His plan or idea. There is nowhere in history where God, Jesus or the Holy spirit called us Christians but we see Jesus calling them "my disciples" meaning scholars or learners, because we were not just to follow Him but to learn from Him. The disciples were first called Christians in Antioch not as a good name but as a way for mocking or insulting them.

(see Acts 11:26 "...And the disciples were called Christians first in Antioch."). kjv

This is only to bring to our attention that we are not just followers but we are to learn from Jesus Christ. The life He lived here on earth is the same life we are to live here on earth if we are true sons of God.

There is a lot to prove that Jesus lived a natural life here on earth just like me and you, yet still He achieved all what He achieved again not because He was anything different from us but because He was strengthened by this spirit life from above. I saw something in the gospel of Luke, which really disturbed me and for some time I really wished it was not there. I honestly had a problem with this until God gave me this revelation of the "Resurrected Life". This is one of those things that make the things of the spirit to appear to be more confusing.

Luke 22:43 "And there appeared an angel unto him from heaven, strengthening him." kjv

Jesus is at Mount of Olives with His disciples praying; and He is asking God to remove a certain cup from Him. Just a verse before this, He told His disciples to pray so that they don't enter into temptation as if He knew His temptation. There were in that prayer for hours, and Jesus kept coming to check on His disciples encouraging them to keep praying. There is nothing much we are given as of the content of the prayer except that He cried unto His Father to remove a certain cup from him but if that's the will of God.

The scripture that we quoted above; the bible is not hesitant to reveal that there was an angel from heaven which came to give Jesus strength. This is where the things of the spirit don't make much sense; I mean, why would Jesus need an angel from heaven to come and give Him strength if there was no room for weakness in him. The way we imagine Jesus to be, the things of the things will not make sense if weakness is to be found in him. Again why would Jesus need an angel to come and strengthen Him, yet Him being Jesus is expected to be above angels in strength.

In defending our faith with the knowledge and imaginations we have of Jesus, how do we explain such scriptures?

These are the kind of scriptures we don't talk much about because they happen to reveal the side of Jesus that we are not willing to accept. When talking about Jesus; the man who walks on water, the man who spoke to the storm and the storm listens, the man who walks to Lazarus burial cave and call Lazarus back to life after days being buried. He being Jesus He does not only resurrect the dead but He Himself is the resurrection and life (*see John11:25*), yet when He was about to face His own death he had serious straggle.

Seeing Jesus straggling with something to an extent whereby He needs external force to give Him strength, it's really becomes difficult to then understand the things of the spirit, because we see Him as one super above all without weakness. I just always wondered what would have happened with Jesus had that angel never came to strengthen Him; you can only imagine.

There is truly nothing disturbing than the way the book of Hebrews put it, because it then reveals something that we don't even imagine to be found in Jesus.

Hebrews 5:7 "When in the days of His flesh, when He had offered up prayers and supplications with strong crying and tears unto Him that was able to save him from death, and was heard in that he feared." kjv

This scripture is now revealing to us why Jesus was praying at Mount of Olives. Jesus was praying to God for Him to save him from death; meaning in as much as Jesus was able to address other people's death, He didn't have enough strength to deal with His own death. This is the worse and most powerful things we'll like to hear about Jesus. It's un-imaginable to count how many times Jesus told his disciples not to fear yet He Himself was once quote in fear and it was recorded in the scripture. The most shocking thing here is that the fear Jesus had wasn't the fear of the Lord but fear of death which was about to befall Him. Paul once said fear is a spirit which doesn't come from God (*see 2Timothy 1:7*), but then to find that same spirit which doesn't come from God in Jesus; Oh! there's truly a lot we are yet to know.

But then the scripture brings it to our understanding that all this happened in the days of His flesh, and this becomes the most powerful thing about the same scripture concerning Jesus. Firstly; the scripture reveals to us that Jesus had His own days of flesh and this justifies to me and you that there were days when Jesus was just human like me and you but yet still He succeed in everything He was to do.

Remember when Jesus was praying on mount olives against His fears and an angel came to strengthen Him, he was about to face the cross or to be crucified; meaning it was the time when He was about to accomplish His mission on earth. If then the scripture says that was at the days of his flesh, then it means everything He did before that time also was in the days of His flesh.

Jesus did all what He did and achieved all He achieved as a natural man who was strengthened by the life from above. He was able to do all the supernatural things He did as a result of living a spirit life in a physical body.

There was a time when Jesus was led by the Holy spirit into the wilderness for a forty days of praying and fasting also to be tempted of the devil (*see Matthew 4:1-11*). There is something I just want you to think about in this scenario; notice that when you read the first verse Jesus is being led by the Holy Spirit into the wilderness, but to my amazement in verse five and verse eight it's no longer the Holy Spirit leading Jesus but the devil. Where was the Holy Spirit when Jesus was now led or taken by the devil? And knowing that the devil is also a spirit, then that makes it's even worse.

Anyways I will just leave that to you to think about it.

All this is not to lower the foundations of our faith but just to prove to us that Jesus walked in this earth just like me and you and He was able to exercise dominion by the help of the greater life from heaven which in our case is the Resurrected Life.

Jesus is not the only man in the scriptures that came from heaven and lived a heavenly life here on earth, but there was another man named John the Baptist. (*See John 1:6 "there was a man sent from God whose named was John."*), knowing where God is; then we can agree that this John was sent from heaven with a heavenly assignment to be executed here on earth and most importantly he was a man not an angel. When you check on how he was born you will notice there are many similarities with the birth of Jesus (*see Luke 1:11-17*). The mother of John" Elisabeth" was barren, but then later an angel appeared to Zacharias the husband with message of joy "thy wife Elisabeth shall bear thee a son, and thou shalt call his name John" and the angel then said he shall be filled with the Holy Ghost and he shall move by the spirit and the power of Elijah. All this makes the life of John to be from above.

It is believed that John the Baptist was Elijah and even Jesus confirmed that which then makes it to be true. Let's then say you don't believe in this resurrected life I'm talking about; how then do you explain John the Baptist being Elijah?

All this is only to prove that there is a life we can live from a world far beyond and above this world; a life that is sponsored from heaven which we can live here on this earth. A life of dominion which is heavenly and we were destined to live long before the creation of man, and this life is called the resurrected life of God. This is the time and season whereby we are to experience this life with awareness such that we can interpret with prove the heart and the mind of God as it is to all the creation.

Our failure in comprehending the spiritual realities has led us into creating ways and formulas in attempting to touch the heart of God yet in the dealings of God with man, we are not at liberty to invent ways into how to worship God but we are shown by Him. We know that the kingdom of God is governed by the kingdom principles of God which makes the possibilities of experiencing God in a deeper dimension and have fruits as by that experience.

So in worshiping God we don't worship according to how we can, but we are to worship Him in His own way and that what makes us to be one with one spirit and one accord. Meaning in as much as we are many different nations submitting to one God under one believe system, we can unite and sound in one voice such that whether you are an African or Asian we will understand and interpret God in one common way.

God has been patient with us for so long, but now we are called into a place of true unity and oneness as the church whereby we can serve God in one common way despite of our nation backgrounds. For so long; we have brought our traditions and attached our different cultures to our worship for God claiming that what makes us who we are, yet unaware we have been limiting the Word of God(Christ) and making it to be without effect in our lives (*see Mark 7:13*). This may be the same reason why we have not been experiencing the greatness of God as the first Church of the apostles did during their time.

It is true that our traditions and cultures are what separate us into these many different beautiful nations and we believe that they make us who we are. The intensity of all these traditions has also played a very big role in causing a division in the church which resulted in many beliefs causing lack of power to the church. The resurrected life is a system provided for us to unity back into one spirit with one voice under one believes system.

Honestly, to God we are supposed to be one despite of our different nationalities. As long as we are baptized by one spirit we are supposed to be one because that same spirit found in all of us must become our new identity making us to be one especially in the eyes of God *(see 1 Corinthians 12:13)*. Such that there is no different difference a Jew or a Gentile but we become one under the same Lord *(see Romans 10:12)*, and this can only be possible if we can all live in this resurrected life of God. This simple mean that in worshiping God we are not to come and continue with our different cultures but we are to come and be given one heavenly culture which will then make us common as the true church of God.

===

Colossians 3:4 "When Christ, who is our life, shall appear, then shall ye also appear with him in glory."

The apostle Paul in this potion of scripture is revealing one more thing we have to check in explaining what this resurrected life is. He is bringing to our understanding a deeper dimension of Christ which has been hidden from the church for a very long time and now it's time for it to be revealed unto the church. Paul is now revealing to us that this Christ is not just a personality but a LIFE, and in his description he says this Christ is our life. There is a dimension of Christ where Christ is not just our Lord. There is a dimension of Christ where He is not just the head of the church while the church being the body. And in this dimension; Christ is the life we live.

In verse three of the same book Paul said *"for you are dead, and your life is with Christ in God"*, so this means that being a dead person you have no life, if you see yourself living it by the means of the life called "Christ". And this is what Paul was trying to explain when he said it's no longer him who lives but the Christ in him (*see Galatians 2:20*). He revealed that as a result of him being crucified with Christ he is dead and him being dead it can't be him living, he then explained that what we see happening; him being alive is by the means of a life called "Christ" which is living inside of him. And the amazing part is that he reveals also that all this is happening while he is still in his flesh.

So Christ is our life and this life is the resurrected life. Remember when Paul said "there is therefore now no condemnation to them which are in Christ Jesus, who walk not after the flesh but after the Spirit" (*see Romans 8:1*). If there can be a possibility that one can be in Christ, then that make Christ a location where people can be or live in.

Number two; those in that location called "Christ" are to "walk" not after the flesh but the Spirit, when you check the word "walk" from the Strongs Bible Version you will notice that it is defined as "to live or deport" meaning those who live not after the flesh but the Spirit. And the spirit in the text is in caps lock meaning it's a noun referring to either a person or a place. So in this text, Paul was referring Christ to a place where we can live or a life that we can live.

In all this we are made to understand that the only way for one to escape condemnation is for that person to be in Christ or to live a Christ life. Knowing that Christ is our life and He is the resurrected life, this content then means to us that we are free from condemnation only when we are living a resurrected life.

Christ is the Resurrected Life we are called to live and it's only in that life we have power over sin and death.

Chapter three

HOW TO RECEIVE THE RSURRECTED LIFE?

You can never live a resurrected life unless you receive it and have proof you have received it. In the captured history of the dealings of God with mankind, there has been many different ways in which this life has been revealed. God has been revealing this life differently depending on who He was dealing with and the time, because in the dealings of God with man it's very important to also consider time. It's true as spirits we come from a world that is not limited by time, but we are to live the life which is above time in a world limited by time and that's why timing becomes very important. Remember different times reveal different possibilities of the same kingdom.

We are talking about a life that is far beyond the limit of time, but yet we are to live that life in a world that is operating under the limit of time. The issue of time is very important even in dealing with the things of the spirit because there are spiritual realities which have changes with time, meaning they are not always applicable but they work depending on the time. There are spiritual realities that God allowed His people to experience as by their time and understanding of Him, meaning He revealed Himself to them in a way that was close to what they were used to so that they can easily understand Him.

This is one of the many reasons why Jesus was to be born of Mary, because if He came in a way far different from mankind we would had a challenge in believing that we can still live that same life He did here on earth.

I know that some of the ways in how to receive this resurrected life has been highlighted before, but now we will be checking them in details. In our attempt to find out how to receive this resurrected life we have to check a bit on the subjects of salvation, being born again, repentance, sanctification and holiness.

From history the message of salvation, repentance and sanctification has always been addressed to mean almost the same thing depending also on the time of event. Depending on which of the two covenants are you addressing theses from; they will give you a different meaning and understanding. Just because we are a new covenant church, I will not focus much on the descriptions of theses from the old covenant perspective but we will focus mostly on how they are addressed on the new covenant age.

> **Repentance:**

The journey of building a relationship with God begins at the level of repentance. Whereby you see the need to change from your ways of doing and conform to a new different way of doing.

Repentance simply means to turn completely from your way to adapt a new or different way; whereby in our content it means to stop living a sinful life and start living a righteous life.

Righteousness in the old covenant is different from righteousness in the new covenant, in the old covenant we have what is called the "self-righteousness" which come by the law and with the new covenant we have "faith righteousness" which come through the faith of Christ (*see Philippians 3:9*).

The self-righteousness is not considered important in the new covenant, but we are expected to have the faith righteousness which is considered to be of God.

The message of repentance is more like you taking that giant step of turning away from your wicked ways or deciding to stop sinning, yet there are dimensions of sin whereby you will need more than repentance to check out of sin. In this kind of a situation it's no longer the person committing sin but the sin itself is manifesting itself through the person (*see Romans7:15-20*). Paul is revealing to us that when you find yourself keep on doing something you don't want to do especially if it sinful; because of consistent repeat of doing that same thing, the spirit of that sin is activated and established in you such that it's no longer you doing that thing but the spirit of that sin in you.

And in such a situation you don't just decide to walk away or stop, but you then need a superior force to help you check out of that situation. So there is a dimension of repentance whereby you don't just decide to stop sinning but you receive a spirit from above which will then help you to stop sinning or repent from your wicked ways. In this dimension, it is God through His Holy Spirit who help you to turn from your wicked ways and start walking in righteousness.

Many people normally choose to call situations where one is not able to easily stop doing something "addiction", yet honestly it more than addiction. It's an activation of the spirit of that same thing because in the world of the spirit everything has a corresponding spirit component. Just like when you pray consistently; you end up activating the spirit of prayer in you such that every time you pray it's no longer just you praying but the spirit of prayer activated in you.

When John the Baptist came, he preached the message of repentance preparing the people for the one to come who was the Christ (see *Acts 19:4*). Notice that even if he baptizes them; they were never really introduced into the kingdom of God until Jesus came who was then to introduce the baptism of the Holy Spirit. Their baptism was only a public declaration to prove that they have turned from their wicked ways.

So this brings us to the understanding that; repentance doesn't make you a son of God, it's simply a step which shows that you are a sinner and you are really willing to change for better. What makes one to be a true son of God is to receive the Holy Spirit of God which will then give you the ability to live a new life "the resurrected life".

➢ **Sanctification and Holiness:**

Sanctification and holiness becomes the process which brings us closer to the image of the Christ, such that we look more like God in every aspect of our lives. The process of sanctification and holiness proofs the completeness of repentance and deliverance and our closeness to the character of the Christ.

Remember; repentance alone doesn't make us to be sons of God and this is where the message of sanctification and holiness comes in.

For some time, I have noticed that our leaders who has attempted to handle the message of sanctification and holiness has focused mostly on what we are separated from or the bad things we stopped to do, yet the backbone of sanctification and holiness is not with what we stopped to do but what we have become after we stopped what we stopped doing.

Sanctification is not just about us separated from sin or sickness, but more about us being drawn closer to Christ after we have been separated from sin and sickness, even death.

For example; if one was having a problem of fornication and gets delivered or repents, that person is not sanctified but only emptied or delivered from that spirit of fornication. If that person is to be sanctified there has to be an infilling after the deliverance has taken place. Meaning there has to be something that occupies the space which was occupied by that fornication spirit after that spirit left.

So the importance of sanctification is not with the worst you used to be, but the more of Christ you have become after you changed from the worst you used to be. This is why it's important for people to get the infilling of the Holy Spirit after a demon has been cast out from them; because if they are left empty, that demon has the right to re-possess that same person over and over again until he/she is filled with the holy spirit. The same goes even with the ministry of healing; when a sickness is removed from a person something must be put in that person to occupy the space which was occupied by that sickness, so that the sickness will not have a chance to come to that same person ever again.

We keep on giving testimonies on how worst we used to be yet the greatest of testimonies is not with how much you have changed, but with how close you are to the character of Christ. The measure of our holiness is not with our inability to sin, but with our closeness to the character of Christ. Many think of sanctification as a religious way of making something holy. Oh No! we don't speak religion here but spirituality. Let it be clearly known that sanctification is not a religious activity of making something or someone holy because there is no holiness with religion, oh yes I repent "there is no holiness with religion". In the new covenant holiness comes spiritually and that's why sanctification is a spiritual activity.

Away with this mentality of thinking that the church is a religious institution. Maybe it was religious before the coming of Jesus Christ, but after the death and resurrection of Jesus Christ the church is a spiritual institution. And this makes Christianity a spiritual fellowship with God, not a religion. Let it be clearly known that all the spiritual things in our fellowship with God are spiritual and not religious.

➢ **Salvation:**

"Can anyone or everyone be saved?"

This is a question I was asked by one of my mentees some years back and at first I thought it's an easy question to answer but then when I started to think about why she asked such a question; I then noticed how difficult that question is.

The most defining moments in a man's life is when one acknowledges the existence of God and see a need of God in his life, just like the greatest achievement one can have is to be called a son of God.

Salvation is a message of deliverance. Mainly in the old covenant the message of salvation was more about God delivering His people from different kinds of bondages yet in the new covenant the message of salvation is mainly for the saving of the soul from eternal death. We are now called unto eternal salvation which is by Christ (*see Hebrews 5:9*) and in as much as this salvation of the lord is show to all men, it doesn't benefit everyone but only those who obey Him.

There was a time in the old when God needed His people who are called by His name to humble themselves, repent and pray seeking His face then

God gives them salvation (*see 2 Chronicles 7:14*). When you check the content of the text, it's more like they were to do something for God to show them salvation yet in our case the salvation is by grace and the love of God for us. Meaning we don't really do much to qualify for the salvation of the Lord but it comes to us as a result of God's love towards us.

Yes, we are now saved not by works but by grace and faith (*see Ephesians 2:8-9*). So salvation to us is a gift from God which is given to us through Christ Jesus. In the olden days' people brought their sacrifices in exchange for their salvation and sanctification yet later we notice that there was really nothing a man could really give which is the value of his redemption (*see Mark 8:37*) and that's why Jesus Christ has to be the absolute sacrifice. The salvation of God is shown to all men, but God never forces His salvation unto man and that is why there is need for one to loudly confess unto salvation (*see Romans 10:10*).

In as much as we receive the salvation of God by grace through faith in Christ Jesus; somehow we have to participate in the process for it to be a success. By our mouth we have to confess unto salvation and by doing so it more like we are taking a step of accepting the salvation of God so that He can then save us.

There is a great need for confession unto salvation to prove that you not ashamed of the Lordship of Jesus Christ and the salvation of God and also to activate the power of salvation unto life because life and death is on the power of the tongue (*see Proverbs 18:21*). The confession is for making a loud declaration even unto every bondage in your life that you are now taking a step unto freedom. The power of salvation gives us the boldness we need to live the life of Christ without fear of anything and is what brings us into the Image of Christ.

Salvation can go a step further, whereby it not just what God can offer but God Himself is salvation (*see Isaiah 12:2*). This level of salvation is applicable when our lives are now hidden in Christ and nothing can harm us because nothing can touch our lives. In such a case Christ in the salvation and the salvation is a place where I live.

There has always been an issue about what Paul said on working out your own salvation (see Philippians 2:12).

When you look closely on this scripture you will notice that Paul was not saying people should come up with their own salvation or putting their own work unto receiving the salvation of God. Many when reading this scripture turn to believe that there is work we have to do in receiving the salvation of God yet that is not true because the salvation of God is not of works but of faith. We don't work to earn the salvation of God, but it is given to us by the grace of God through faith in Christ Jesus.

The apostle Paul was outlining to the church that there is need for one to show the fruit of salvation for their salvation to be visible to men and even to God. If there is nothing to prove that we are saved, then how are we different from those who are not saved? So here the apostle was talking about the actions as a result of receiving salvation, just like faith without works is dead (*see James2:26*). We are to work to show our salvation and that's what makes us different from those who are not in salvation. There has to be a way to prove our salvation such that we differ from those who are not saved. This is through the fruits of salvation and this is what "working out your salvation" means.

Let the message of salvation be preached with revelation, such that we don't full ourselves into thinking that we have been saved yet there are no works to support our salvation. If we claim we are saved, then there has to be something which prove that we are now different from those not saved. The testimony of our salvation is with the ability of attaining things which those who are not saved can't attain.

As long as we have the same testimony with those who have not received the salvation of the Lord, then it's a lie to confess that we have received the salvation of the Lord. This brings us to the conclusion; there has to be fruits of our salvation to serve as evidence to prove our salvation to our generation and event God. And we call this "working out your salvation".

➤ Born-Again:

The message of being born-again has remained a mystery for a very long time. As Christians we confess almost each and every day that we are born-again. Honestly it has become a habit that we believe differs us from those we believe have not yet been saved by God through Jesus Christ. But as for me I have always wondered; are we really born again? One may say; depending on the knowledge and understanding we have of being born-again, we can say we are born-again. If we are to define the nature of being born-again by our definition for "being born-again", then we must have a common understanding of what it is to be born again.

What is really to be born-again?

Many sermons have been given and many books have been written in attempt to tackle the topic of being born-again. Many preachers, teachers and scholars of the bible have even invented ways and steps into being born-again. And these has played a very important role in giving us a picture of what it is to be born-again. Remember we are trying to have assurance on whether we are truly born-again or we are only convincing ourselves that we are born-again.

It is believed that being born-again means giving up your old life to live a new life through Christ Jesus, particular in evangelism to refer to "spiritual rebirth". I also believe this is sensibly true, but only if we can explain in details this new life and how we can really attain it, because we can never live a new life unless somehow we have received it. Again, let us not forget that being born again was never the original plan of God about mankind, but it's a system that came later as a result of man falling from the grace and glory of God (*see Romans 3:23 "For all have sinned, and come short of the glory of God," kjv*).

As a result of falling in short of the glory of God, we found ourselves in sin and we know; it's by one man's sin that all men are born in sinful nature (*see Romans 5:12*), and that's the main reason rebirth was then necessary.

Because of sinful nature, men are born of a corruptible seed and the system of being born-again is what then gives us the ability to be born of an incorruptible seed by the word of God which lives and abide forever (*see 1 Peter 1:23*).

It will be very important to go to the origin of the term "born-again" if we are to truly find the true meaning of being born-again. The first time we hear of the term "born-again" it was by Jesus Christ himself when He was talking to a Jewish leader by the name Nicodemus in the gospel of John.

John 3:3 "Jesus answered and said unto him, verily, verily, I say unto thee, Except a man be born again, he cannot see the kingdom of God." Kjv.

If you can notice, the message of Jesus to this Jewish leader was not about faith and believe but strictly on accessing the kingdom of God. There is a possibility that one can believe in God but not have access to the kingdom of God, just like what Jesus said about not everyone calling unto His name shall enter the kingdom of Heaven (*see Matthew 7:21*).

Looking at the personality of Nicodemus, you will notice that he was a member of the church council at that time, yet there was still need for him to be born-again if he was to enter into the kingdom of God. Firstly, this tells us that there is a great difference between believing in God and being born-again.

If people that are in believe and fellowship are still expected to be born-again then what it is really to be born-again? People that are in fellowship especially about God, they are expected to have given up their old life to live a new life but then how is it that they are still expected to be born-again. This outline to us that there is more in being born-again than what we already know from all our studies and understanding.

In the conversation between Jesus and Nicodemus of being born-again, there was a lot Nicodemus never really straight away understood and that's why Jesus kept on explaining to him what He was trying to teach him about being born again. In the content of Jesus message, Jesus made it clear that the "again" was not in form of repetition as Nicodemus was thinking.

Knowing that the gospel of John was written in Koine Greek, the original translation of the "again" is "from above or from the beginning". So this means Jesus actually said to Nicodemus "except a man is born from above or beginning, he cannot see the kingdom of God".

Some bible translations like the King James Version, NIV, ESV and the NLT use "born again" while some like the New English Translation, the MSG bible and the Amplified Bible use "from above". So we can agree on the fact that the term "born-again" means to be "born from above" implying "from Heaven".

Even with such content, Nicodemus still never understood until Jesus used the subject of baptism to explain what He meant. In verse five Jesus said "verily, verily, I say unto thee, except a man is born of water and of the spirit he cannot enter the kingdom of God". This is how being born-again is attached with baptism and is the principle which gives us access to the resurrected life. So the principle of baptism is what opens the door unto being born-again, especially if it is applied correctly. And this same principle of baptism becomes the door way into receiving the resurrected life. Remember, we access the Kingdom of God only when we have under-go the process of baptism; both the water and the spirit baptism.

The water baptism plays a very important role in our fellowship and relationship with God. The water baptism of John was more of a public announcement to proof one's repentance from his/her wrong doings, yet after the death and resurrection of Jesus Christ; water baptism it symbolizes believe and involvement to the death and resurrection of Jesus Christ. When we are immersed in the water; we are being buried with Jesus and when we arise from the water we are being raised with Him into becoming a new creature (*see Colossians 2:12*).

In this process of water baptism, you are to be immersed once and rise all at once, not three times. I noticed that there are some who immerse people three time in the water when conducting the water baptism, and this is mostly because they baptize in the name of the Father, the Son and the Holy Spirit.

If the water baptism represents our communion and fellowship in the death and resurrection of Jesus Christ, then we are to be immersed once since Jesus died and was raised only once. It is true they were to be baptized in the name of the Father, the Son and the Holy spirit and later it was said they are to be baptized in the name of the Lord, but finally the Lord was revealed and His name is Jesus Christ. So this means we are to be baptized in the name of Jesus who is our Lord and savior. Let us conducts our water baptism with revelation; water baptism must be conducted in the name of Jesus if it is to symbolize our fellowship in the death of Jesus Christ.

There is also the baptism of the Holy Spirit which is supposed to be conducted almost exactly after you have given your life to Jesus Christ or after you have received the water baptism. The message of the spirit baptism was first preach by John the Baptist as he was preparing the way for the revelation of Jesus the Christ. He indicated that he was only baptizing people with water but there is someone coming after him who was to baptize people with the holy Ghost (*see Mark 1:9*). The baptism of the Spirit is very important in building and confirming a true relationship with God because it is the element which proves if we are really sons of God or not (*see Romans 8:14*).

The baptism of the spirit is what conforms us to the image of the Christ and brings us into oneness and one body as believers such that there is no difference of race or nationality (*see 1 Corinthians 12:13*). The Holy Spirit is the personality of both Jesus and God the Father all together in one form. And this is why it's very important to receive the baptism of the spirit if we are to truly know the fullness of God. The work of the Holy Spirit is beyond words explanation, but above all; it is what gives us the life which God has predestined us for, long before the foundations of the earth.

According to Jesus; we should never go into ministry or working for/with God without the baptism of the Holy Spirit, because the Holy Spirit is the only element which proofs and demonstrate that God is with us. And this is the same reason why even after He has taught His disciples almost everything, He still insisted that they remain in Jerusalem until they were baptized with the Holy Ghost. This is the reason why we should never find ourselves doing any work of ministry without the infilling of the Holy Spirit.

How amazing it is that in our days we do find ourselves working in the house of God without the infilling of the holy Spirit?

The journey with God is impossible unless you are baptized with the spirit. So above all things we should desire the baptism of the spirit with the evidence of speaking in tongues (*see Acts 2:3-11,*

Acts 10:46 and Acts 19:6). This is because it is in the baptism of the Holy Spirit where we receive the life that is greater (resurrected life) and get to commune with God in the spirit realm with evidence. We know that God is spirit and those worshiping Him must conduct their worship in the spirit; so if we don't have the spirit in us, how can we say we are in true worship and fellowship with God?

John 4:24 "God is a Spirit: and they that worship Him must worship Him in spirit and in truth." kjv.

Such a scripture makes it clear that it's only in the spirit where one can truly worship God, making it impossible to worship God if you're not in the spirit. So if we say we are worshiping God yet we have not received the Spirit then we are fulling ourselves because it's only through the Spirit that we can truly worship God. This is why the baptism of the Holy Spirit is very important in building a relationship with God. There is truly no journey with God without the Holy Spirit.

===

What does it mean to receive Jesus Christ into your life?

Some like to interpret "being born-again" as receiving Jesus Christ in your life as your lord and savior. Yes, this is true; but then what does "receiving Jesus Christ" means? Depending on our different level of understanding the things of the spirit, we define "receiving Jesus Christ" differently. Some uses the confession of the Lordship of Jesus Christ just like what Paul taught the church in Roman that a man can confess the lord Jesus and believe his way into salvation (see Romans 10:9-10).

In the attempt to receive Jesus Christ, we have even invented prayers unto salvation like "Lord Jesus, I believe in you, come into my life and forgive my sins...". What does it mean to "come into my life"? Honestly, Jesus is sited at that right hand side of the Father (see Colossians 3:1) and what is in service right now is not Him in person but the Holy Spirit. So by inviting Jesus into our lives, we are actually inviting the Christ which is the spirit of God that will teach us everything and bring to our remembrance all what Jesus has taught (*see John 14:26*).

So the phrase "receiving Jesus Christ" simply means to receive the Spirit from above which will then give us an experience of the heavenly life and confirm our fellowship with God as our Father. And this is what being born again is to the new covenant church. When we pray for Jesus to come into our lives; we are actually asking for the Christ (holy spirit) to come and take over roll control in our lives. It's a moment of appreciating that we do not sustain enough intelligence on our own and so we need a supreme help from above.

It is in this moment whereby we should be receiving the holy spirit to help us to live in the newness of life just like Jesus during the days of His flesh here on earth. And this is the only way we can truly be conformed into the image of the Christ.

====

If being born again truly means exactly what is means; then we owe it to ourselves to ask the question "are we truly born-again?"

This is honestly not to make our lives difficult or to bring fear into our position of faith, but only to bring us to a place of assurance of what we say we are and what we believe in. It's very important to be sure of our standing with God such that we are not caught by surprise at a time where there will be no more turning back.

As it was highlighted earlier; being born-again is just to be born from above (meaning from heaven) and this happens through the principle of baptism. In this principle of baptism, is where we are buried with Jesus and be raised with Him while we receive a life from above to possess our fleshly life such that we can live a life higher than the one we lived before. So, the "born from heaven" it is coming of the heavenly life into our physical body to give us the ability to live a heavenly life here on earth as it is in heaven. And there is no need for a physical death for one to experience this heavenly life.

So we receive the resurrected life through the principle of being born again and this becomes the beginning of our journey and fellowship with God as true sons of God. The greatest transformation a man can have is to be born again and receive the Christ life which gives the power to do business with God and rule as God has instructed.

This resurrected life becomes the answer to most of the question we always had about God and His plan for mankind and the universe. Even unlocking the promises of God is hidden in the mystery behind this resurrected life.

Remember, God has blessed us with all the spiritual blessings in the heavenly place in Christ (*see Ephesians 1:3*). One may ask, why we don't see or experience all these blessings given to us by God? Well; if you can notice, these blessings are not everywhere but are in a specific location "in Christ" and that's mean you can only access them when you are in that location.

This Christ is our life (*see Colossians 3:1*), the life we receive from above through the principle of spiritual baptism. If this Christ is our life and God has placed our blessings in Christ; then it's only in the resurrected life, we can truly access the blessings and promises of God.

The resurrected life is the greatest gift ever given to mankind by God, because it interprets the true nature of God to His creation. The resurrected life brings to our understanding the power and the love of God in its true form.

The Power and the Love of God is what gives true meaning to the message that will sustain the church. This mean that; without the power of God, any message we preach is empty, yet without the Love of God we have no message at all. That's why there is great need for power and the love of God if we are to succeed as the current church of God.

The resurrected life is what gives birth to the love we need to have a message and the power we need to demonstrate our message for it to truly sustain the church. Receive the resurrected life and experience unspeakable joy, peace and love from God.

Chapter four

TRUE FELLOWSHIP WITH GOD

Many still believes that Christianity is a religion just because they think there is no better way to define Christianity without attaching it to religion. You know; a billion people can believe a lie to be truth but that will never really convert that same lie to be truth no matter how many people believes it to be truth. The nature of Christianity doesn't allow it to fall under religious institution, no matter how hard we can convince each other into believing that it is a religion.

I know; everyone is entitled to his/her own belief but that doesn't make every belief to be true. Just like if one kills a person and find good lawyers to defend him even to a point where he is found not guilty of the charge; still that will never change the fact that he did killed the person regardless of the court decision.

If you can do a study on what qualifies a practice to be a religion, you will notice that Christianity will never qualifies to be a religion. But again we can call it whatsoever we want; that will never change it truthful nature.

Personally I believe, to us as Christians; Christianity should never be considered as one of those religions out there, but it should be seen as a spiritual fellowship with God. To be called a Christian should be as a result of looking and behaving more like Christ Jesus. We shouldn't be called Christians just by following Jesus but by receiving the same spirit (Christ) He received.

Because when you check back on the origin of the name "Christians", you will notice that the disciples of Jesus were first called Christians in Antioch because they looked like Jesus and have received the same spirit Jesus received, which is called "the Christ".

Maybe we have not be experiencing the full potential of Christianity because we have been believing it to be something different from what it is. Let us teach ourselves to accept and believe Christianity to be what it was made to be. In short, Christianity is the fellowship with God through Christ.

===

1 Corinthians 1:9 "God is faithful, by whom ye were called unto the fellowship of his Son Jesus Christ our Lord" kjv

When God said "let us make man in our own image, after our likeness" it's clear he needed something to look and behave like Him, and even carry His agenda of dominion on earth. So the vision of God for mankind was and still is to look and behave like God, and execute God's will here on earth as it is in heaven. All this was to be possible because man was supposed to be always in "Eden" which spiritually symbolizes the presence of God.

But because of the introduction of sin and the fall of man, we were separated from our rightful

113

position of being in the presence of God. As a result of this separation, we started experiencing hardship and impossibilities which we would have never knew if man remained in the presence of God. So the calling back to God is as a result of having left the presence of God.

By the faithfulness and kindness of God; even when we were far from the presence of God, the love of God still reached unto us to call us back to our rightful position where we have the image of God and authority over everything on earth.

Through His son, God called us back into His presence where we have fellowship with Him as our Father. And this is why we should understand that we are not called into religion but we are called into fellowship where the love of God is the life we live. When you reduce the call of God to religion, there is a lot of the kingdom possibilities you will never experience in your life time. The call of God is not religious but a call unto fellowship through Christ Jesus.

For any fellowship to be a success, there is a great need for faithfulness which always comes with loyalty. This applies even for our fellowship with God; it can never be a success if there is no faithfulness from both parties meaning "God and the church".

The apostle Paul in the scripture quoted above, is making it clear that God has and is perfectly playing His part of faithfulness in this fellowship we have with Him. When you notice, Paul didn't say God was or He will be faithful but he said "God is faithful". This means that the faithfulness of God is not affected by time, it is always current whether you in the pass, in the now or in the future. In simpler terms, this means "God is forever faithful".

If God is forever faithful then there is no need for us to question His faithfulness over us, the only faithfulness to be questioned here is ours as the church. Are we faithful enough to hold on to the profession of faith?

Let it be known that in this fellowship with God, faithfulness is not a choice but a requirement. It is expected of us to be always found faithful if this fellowship will stand successfully (*see 1Corinthians*

4:2). So whether you can or not, whether you want or not; you are not at liberty to choose but it's a requirement to be found forever faithful just like God is forever faithful.

===

In my years of studying scriptures, I've noticed many different kinds of relationships God had with many different individuals and groups of people. From the days of the old covenant all through to the days of the new covenant, we see God having different kinds of fellowships with His people in different many ways. Even so; I believe there is a common fellowship we can all have with God such that we can all reach into oneness with God and confess the same words of Jesus Christ "I and my Father are one".

With all the fellowships God had with His people from the past until now, there is one outstanding character that really caught my attention. There is a man in the old who walked with God and as a result of his fellowship with God, he experienced something that Jesus talk about when He was about to raise Lazarus from the dead.

Lazarus who is believed to be a friend of Jesus was once sick and Jesus was told to come and heal him, unfortunately fortunately Jesus delayed until Lazarus died. So when Jesus was now coming, he wasn't just coming to heal a sick man but to raise a dead man being four days buried. After all; in the world of Jesus, death is still a sickness which can be healed.

Finding them troubled, He introduced himself by saying he is the resurrection and life. (*see John 11:22-28*) Notice that Jesus is referring Himself as resurrection and life, meaning having him (Jesus) in you is having resurrection and life. He then said those who have died believing in Him shall be raised back to life again. I guess people believed that because the message of resurrection was already preached before.

The problem was with the statement He then said in verse 26," And whosoever liveth and believeth in me shall never die. Believest thou this? kjv"

Jesus said something which even up to now we still have a challenge to understand and believe. Jesus said if you are alive and believe in him you shall never die, and if you check the content; Jesus is not talking about a spiritual death as many would like to say, but He is talking about a physical death right at the time when he was about to raise a man that has died physically. In terms of spiritual death, I believe they were all dead because at that time they had not yet received the spirit of live (Christ).

If Jesus means exactly what he is saying, then why prepare for death when we're still alive and believe in Christ Jesus?

Anyways; my comment is on Enoch, who is said to have been in a good fellowship with God which resulted in him not experiencing death (*see Hebrews 11:5*).

The bible is not hesitant to attest of the fact that there was a man who walked with God and his faith grew to a level whereby he should not see death. God took him and we are told that before he was taken, he had a testimony that he pleased

God. You don't really see such testimonies in the scriptures, whereby a man of God can testify of a relationship another man of God had with God. Remember, Moses also testified of the relationship Enoch had with God and also attest on the fact that Enoch never saw death (*see Genesis 5:24*).

Truly, this Enoch must have been a very outstanding character to have other men of God attesting of his relationship with God. After all; he experienced what Jesus talked about when He was about to raise Lazarus from the dead. And all this now, it's proof to us that there is a level of fellowship with God whereby it becomes impossible to experience death. Yes, I have said it! There is a way we can fellowship with God such that we live a life above the reach of death.

Unfortunately, we are not told much about this Enoch from the bible we now have, except that he had a great relationship with God. Personally I would love to know in details the kind of fellowship this man had with God which qualified him to escape the grip of death. I have always wondered on how was he different from us, because with the little information we have about him; it's clear he lived an earthly life with earth needs yet still he was able to have a testimony that he pleased God to a degree that he shouldn't experience death.

I know, there are many different kinds of graces allocated for body of Christ which sometimes make us to experience different possibilities of the same God; fellowship is not one of the graces allocated but a calling for all who believes in God through Christ Jesus. If the experience of Enoch was as a result of his fellowship with God, then he can't be the only one to escape the grip of death. I understand, even the prophet Elijah was also taken into heaven without experiencing death but then again, what would they have done which we can't do now.

The truth is; we can't be in true fellowship with God and be in fear of death at the same time. Remember, we fellowship with God in His presence where His love is perfected and we already know that where love is perfected there is no fear (*see 1 John 4:18*).

In *John 10:10*, Jesus is making it know unto us His assignment here on earth. He puts it straight and clear that he has come so that we might have live and have it more abundantly. Jesus is first making it clear that in as much as He is coming, he's not the only one who has come. There is a different being who has come with a different agenda yet as of Him, He came that we might have live and have it in abundance. Come to think of it; why would Jesus speak of abundant life if all life comes in abundance? To me this is prove that there is a life higher and far greater than the life we have seen and this life is attained by the coming of Jesus.

True fellowship with God is in living the abundance life where there is no fear or death. Unless and until we all live the resurrected life of Christ we can never say we are in true fellowship with God. We know that true fellowship with God is only possible when one has overcome the sinful nature and its darkness, and living above sin and darkness is only possible if we are living the resurrected life of Christ.

To say you are in fellowship with God and to be actually in fellowship with God are two different things, just like saying you are a Christian and to be truly a Christian. If to be a Christian is measured by our closeness to the character of Christ, then how many of all those who call themselves Christians are really Christians?

Being in a true fellowship with God is measured by our ability to remain in light and show no symptoms of darkness. It will truly be a lie to say we are in fellowship with God while we walk in darkness *(see 1 John 1:6-7)*, yet when we walk in light then we are where He is.

By our own wisdom and strength, we can never escape the darkness of this world, and that's why the resurrected life is the only way out from the darkness of this world. Remember, in the resurrected life we live the life of Christ in Christ where Christ becomes our light in the midst of every darkness. Meaning, outside of Christ is darkness and light is only experienced in Christ.

This is more like what happened in Egypt when God was bringing deliverance to the children of Israel who were held captive by Pharaoh. When you read the book of *Exodus 10:21-23*, God is instructing Moses to stretch forth his hand towards heaven such that there can be thick darkness all over the land of Egypt.

And actually Moses did stretch his hand and there was thick darkness which covered the whole land of Egypt. For about three days there was no movement in the land of Egypt, yet the bible goes on to reveal that in the dwellings of the children of Israel there was light. Let's not forget the dwellings of the children of Israel was in Goshen which was in the land of Egypt. If the darkness covered all the land of Egypt, then Goshen should have been covered also since it was in Egypt.

So how did the children of Israel have light while everywhere else there was thick darkness?

There are many different understandings around this matter, again depending on the revelation we carry.

Some years back I once had a pastor by name "Emmanuel Makandiwa" teaching on this matter and he highlighted something which really caught my attention. He said "If that light was visible to everyone, the people in Egypt should have made their way toward Goshen where there was light" and this made me to wonder what kind of light was in Goshen. In his distribution, he continued and said "it might have been that God have upgraded the sight of the Israelites to see in the midst of that darkness".

If it's true that the darkness covered the whole land of Egypt, that should include the dwellings of the Israelites. Then how was it that they still experienced light when everyone else was in darkness? It is clear to me that the darkness covered every place in Egypt, but only those who were in the presence of God did not experience the darkness because there is no darkness in His presence. I believe God was their light in that darkness, just like Christ is our light in this world full of darkness. It is only in Christ we can truly experience light and be in true fellowship with God.

When we are in Christ and have His life as our light, we then become the light ourselves. Jesus once said we are the light of this world and this is as a result of being with Him (*see Matthew 5:14*). This means that the life of Christ will begin to shine in us such that the world will then experience the light of God through us as the true sons of God. Living a resurrected life is what conforms us into becoming what Christ Jesus is and people can experience God through us.

We are all called into fellowship with God through Christ Jesus who is our Lord and savior, and true fellowship with God is through living a resurrected life which is the Christ life.

CONCLUSION

Acts 10:38 "How God anointed Jesus of Nazareth with the Holy Ghost and with power: who went about doing good, and healing all that were oppressed of the devil; for God was with him" kjv.

God's plan for mankind has never changed and will never change. It is still the Will of God for mankind to rule earth and bring the heavenly culture here on earth as it is in heaven.

The greatest testimony we have as the church is the success of Jesus Christ in His mission which then brought many into fellowship with God. If it was not of the obedience and perseverance of Jesus Christ in His mission, we would have remained foreigners in the kingdom of God. Thanks be to God who gave Jesus the strength and power he needed to succeed with His mission. The message of the success of Jesus of Nazareth has been the power which has brought many into true fellowship with God since the first church until today.

Just like how Peter stood up and testified on how God anointed Jesus of Nazareth with the Holy Ghost and with power to go about doing the business of God with power. It's clear that Jesus succeeded in His mission because God was with him. Jesus never succeeded by his own strength or wisdom but by the presence of God which was always with Him. He succeeded because God anointed him with the Holy Ghost and with power which then made him to be superior then any situation he faced.

We are never supposed to go about doing the business of God unless we are empowered for that kind of business. Let's get the same empowerment Jesus got otherwise we will misrepresent the kingdom of God to our generation.

The testimony of our Christianity is not with what we say about God, but what we do as result of having Him on our side. Jesus went about doing good and healing all those who were oppressed of the devil just because God was with him. If we are to truly overcome the devil, we must understand that it will take more than just words we can speak; there is need for the Holy Ghost and power to truly conquer the work of the devil. If we have no power, we can never represent the kingdom of God because the kingdom of God is not in words but in the demonstration of the Holy Spirit and power *(see 1 Corinthians 4:29)*. The resurrected life is what gives us the power we need to successfully represent the kingdom of God in its true nature.

Paul once said he can do all things through Christ who strengthen him *(see Philippians 4:13)*. This is very real and true; we can do all thing only if we can be in Christ because the possibility of experiencing a life without impossibilities is in Christ. We have been given a chance to live a life with no limitations and this life is called the resurrected life of Christ.

This resurrected life is the door way into unlocking the promises of God we have been waiting for all long. If man like Paul experienced this life and even had a testimony while they were still on earth, we can also experience this greater life and have evidence of our daily fellowship with God.

I know there are many out there who are experiencing this greater life, but I believe it's high time we experience it collectively as the church. Whereby every believer can bring to manifestation if possibly all the possibilities of the kingdom of God. Most of what we do and experience as believers is what is in parts; It's time we experience that which is perfect. Just like what Paul said about the knowledge we have that it will always be in parts until that which is perfect comes *(see 1 Corinthians 13:9-10)*.

Living a resurrected life is having a chance to experience the heavenly life here on earth as it is in heaven. We live in such a time where God doesn't reveal Himself to anyone but only His sons. No one knows the father more than the son and no one knows the son more than the father; this communion is what make the father and the son to be one. We are only brought into true fellowship with God as sons by the Holy Spirit.

It's only when we are led by the spirit that we have the qualification to have the revelation of the Christ which makes us to become sons of God (*see Romans 8:14*).

We can all believe in God but that doesn't mean we all belong to Him; only those who have the Spirit of Christ belongs to Christ (*see Romans 8:9*). And this is why the resurrected life is very important; it gives us the heavenly identity. Access to heaven is given to only those who have the heavenly identity in them which is the spirit of Christ. Let our greatest desire be to look more like God in every detail of our lives and to host His presence here on earth as it is in heaven.

This can only be possible when it's no longer us who lives but the Christ manifesting himself through us. This is a call to the restoration of the true church of Christ where Christ is the head and the church is the body and all thing are put under the feet of Jesus which is the church.

Living a resurrected life helps us to transform our lives into the living epistle God wants us to be (*see 2 Corinthians 3:2-6*). Paul in this scripture is making it clear to us that we have been made ministers of the new testament; not of letter or written words but of spirit because anything that is not of the spirit kills yet the spirit gives life. He is also revealing that the dealings and expectation of God for man are no longer written with ink, but with Spirit and not on tables of stone, but in the hearts of man; meaning that the dealings of God with man are now personal, spiritual and internal affairs.

We are to live a life worthy of the calling we have received (*see Ephesians 4:1*) because we no longer live for ourselves but for the one who died and was raised for us. We are made witnesses of the perfect love of God demonstrated to this world with power, and our testimony is not in words but in the demonstration of the spirit of the living God. The value of our testimony is not with what we can say about God, but with how much of God is revealed through our lives. We have talked much about God; it's time we demonstrate Him to our generation with unquestionable evidence from eternity.

The resurrected life is what keeps us in the presence of the Father to enjoy the abundant life God has given us. Remember outside the presence of God there is no life, but only those in the presence of God can experience the life of Christ.

===

Just like the parable of the prodigal son Jesus told in the book of *Luke 15:11-32*. This story was to teach on the importance of fellowship between God and the church. The father had two sons as we now the story; the younger son came to the Father and demanded a portion of his birth-right and the father gave him. The younger son then went his way to squander all what he got from the father, while the elder son remained with the father. Honestly, this is what is happening even up to today; many come to God and ask of anything and when they get it they check out from the presence of God.

People come to God because of what He can do for them, yet we are supposed to come to Him because of Who He is, not what He can do. God was God long before He even created anything. So the creation doesn't make Him to be God but He created because He is God.

The portion run out and this younger son came back to his senses and returned back to the father to ask for forgiveness.

God is ready to give us what so ever we ask of Him. But let this be a learn to all; what we get from God is sustained by God, meaning; the blessings of God remain a blessing for as long as you are in the presence of God, but when you check out from the presence of God that same blessing can turn into a case. We can ask from God anything we desire and get it, but we should know that its durability is with Him as the giver. After all; it takes higher wisdom to know that it's better to have God than to have what He can provide.

The father kindly welcomed him back and even celebrated his return back home with great joy and love. I know many choose to focus on the wrong deeds of the younger son which then drives them away from the bigger picture of the story. The story was told to bring a lesson on fellowship between the Father and His sons, and the benefits of being in true fellowship with the Father.

As the father was celebrating the return of the lost son, the elder son who was always with the father was not happy about the celebration of his prodigal brother. This might be one of the many reasons why the church is not growing fruitfully. We are not very much welcoming to our brothers and sisters who have not been in good terms with God. And by this action we are no different from them because such action shows that in as much as we are with the father we still carry a different mindset and we don't have the love of the Father in us.

The elder son started to complain to the father about him serving the father without disobeying his father's command yet he was never given anything to go and enjoy with his friends. He's now revealing that in as much as he is with the father; the intentions of being given something to go and enjoy with his friends was there and this makes him no different from his brother.

This really opened my eyes into seeing that we can be with the Father and not be in true fellowship with Him, because when we are in true fellowship with God; we are to understand the mind of God and interpret the heart of God as it is. Just like what Paul said "let the mind of Christ be in you" (*see Philippians 2:5*)

The response of the father in verse 31 becomes the key to true fellowship with the father. The father said "son, you are always with me, and all that is mine is yours" and he then spoke of the importance of celebrating the brother who was dead and has just came back to life. The father revealed something very important in fellowship; as sons who are with the father, everything of the father is ours for so long as we are with him. How powerful this is? For as long as I'm with the Father, I need not to worry about anything because having the Father is having everything of the Father. This is the power we are invited into, whereby we live a life of all the possibilities of God with no limits.

===

Living a resurrected life gives us the ability to live our lives and succeed as if the devil does not exist. James once said there is a way we can submit to God and resist the devil such that the devil will be running away from us (*see James 4:7*). The writer is revealing to us that there is a way we can be connected to God such that we have no time to entertain the devil and as a result he will flee from us. Logically, we have never imagined a situation whereby the devil runs away as a result of our arrival yet it is very true; there is a level of alinement with God which makes us not just to be afraid of the devil but the devil will be afraid of us.

Just like what happened with Jesus and the man with legion of demons in *Luke 8:26-33*; Jesus is just arriving in the country of Gadarenes and He meet a man with devils. When the man with the devils saw Jesus, he cried out and fell down before Jesus and began to cried for mercy. Notice, at the time Jesus has not said anything yet these devils recognize Jesus as a Son of God and they are ready to check out of the man without Jesus casting them out.

This is being an authority in the spirit, whereby you have your name registered in the spirit and the devil have no choice but to honor your presence. I call this "being a problem to your problem".

If the devil has been a problem to you; that's changing today, you will become a problem to the devil and every other problem as long as you attain this resurrected life of Christ.

God will never instruct us to seek something we cannot find. This life is very true and it can be a reality in our lives. When Jesus is teaching us to seek the kingdom of God and all other thing shall be added, it because the kingdom can be found. I have made this a reality in my life and now I speak with evidence that the kingdom can be found and when you have found it, you will notice that every other thing you need is truly added as you walk by the principles of the kingdom.

Actually, according to Jesus; as children of God, we should not be worried about the same things the world is worried about because the Father who is in heaven knows that we need those things (*see*

Matthew 6:30-34). There is a way on how God has provided for us as His sons, such that we don't find ourselves equally worried as the world is. The reality of the gospel of Jesus Christ supposed to bring peace to us even in the midst of deep troubles, because for as long as He is God we have our hope. Our hope is not in what He can do, but it is in the fact that He is God and He is our Hope.

===

Now we know that we receive this resurrected life of Christ through the principle of baptism (both the water and the spirit baptism), whereby we die and are buried with Jesus to be risen again with Christ into the newness of life. There is an expectation by heaven for us to live in the resurrected life equipped by the same spirit which raised Jesus from the dead. The expectation comes with actions to prove that we were raised with Christ from the dead.

Colossians 3:1-2 "if ye then be risen with Christ, seek those things which are above, where Christ sitteth on the right hand of God. Set your affection on things above, not on things on the earth." Kjv.

The apostle Paul is now bringing to our attention that if it's true that we have been raised with Christ then there has to be a change in our desires and affections. We are to seek those things which are heavenly supplied and set our affection on things above, not on things on the earth. Yes! This is very true and possible; remember when we receive the Christ life we receive a heavenly life, so how can we satisfy a heavenly life with earthly things. We can have proof to ourselves and those around us that we now live a superior life by changing our desires from being earthly to be heavenly.

You can do a checkup; on all the things you desire in life, which of them are heavenly supplied? If all your desires are heavenly supplied, then you are sure you were truly raised with Christ.

Not that all earthly things are bad. We still have to live here on earth so we need earthly things to make a living here on earth, but the idea here is not to set our affection on those earthly things because they are supposed to be supplied to us by the principle of seeking and finding the kingdom of God. God has already provided all the things which pertains to life and Godliness through the revelation we have of Christ (*see 2 Peter 1:3*), so we only find Christ and have all we need.

Our life is hidden with Christ in heaven, so we live it from heaven were we already have our victory over everything we encounter.

The only way to desire what is in heaven is when you know the things which are in heaven, and the ability to know the things which are in heaven is given to the heavenly life we live from heaven. In as much as we are many different denominations; this resurrected life is the key to unite us back into one church of Christ with one Spirit.

This resurrected life is an investment to the manifestation of the true church of God (the body of Christ) which will know and understand the mind and the heart of God. This is a chance for the church to bring into reality the possibilities of God to our experience with true evidence. Through this life of Christ, we can have our testimony of being born again with evidence to our generation to support and prove that what we believe in is very true and practical. This is God's desire and ultimate gift to the world such that there will be no much different between heaven and earth.

===

Finally, if we will lack prayer; all this will just end at a level of being stories yet for it to be a reality there is much sacrifice and dedication of prayer needed. Prayer is the key to unlock the spiritual realities. I know; many have reduced prayer into just a communication with God, and that's the reason why they don't experience much of the spiritual realities. Even if you are to believe prayer to be a communication between man and God, you also have to understand that it's a two-way communication. Meaning it can't be you talking all the time, but you talk to God and God has to talk back to you. Either way; what we keep doing and call it prayer is somehow questionable.

Through biblical exegesis; we came up with many different types of prayer, including: worship and praise prayer, supplication prayer, thanksgiving prayer, petition and intercession prayer and spiritual warfare prayers. You see; even if we can agree that these are the types of prayers we have, they still can't be administered the same way if they are to mean and address different situations.

The revelation and understanding of prayer you have will be your limit to what you can experience in/through prayer. I'm not trying to erase what we already know about prayer, but just saying there are deeper dimensions of prayer more than what we can just say. There is a dimension of prayer where you commune with God in such a way that you understand everything God is saying even when He is quiet, and also God will be receiving everything you are saying while you are actually not saying anything. We call this dimension "the intimacy fellowship" with God. It's only in this kind of prayer you can interpret the mind and the heart of God.

There is something outstanding I saw in the book of *Genesis 8:21* which can help to support this dimension of prayer. More than just the message

Moses in giving us, I noticed that Moses was giving us a message from the LORD yet that LORD never spoke that message to anyone but only to Himself *(and the LORD said in His heart…)*.

Honestly I can respect the message but my question here is; how did Moses get to know what God is saying in His heart?

If the names of animals Adam gave to the animals was what was in God's mind, then what do we call that?

This is revealing to us that you can hear what God has not yet said verbally, and this is far beyond prophecy. In *Isaiah 14:12-13*, we also here the prophet telling us about something the devil only said in His heart, yet it was detected and recorded. There are deeper dimensions of prayer than just to kneel down and speak to God.

There is a dimension of prayer where prayer is not just what you do, but you "yourself" becomes a place where prayer is fermented. Remember; God once declared through the prophet Isaiah that "my house shall be called a house of prayer" (*see Isaiah 56:7*). And Jesus also quoted the same scripture in Mark 11:17 which then establish whatsoever the prophet Isaiah said. The scripture is actually revealing to us that as for the house of God, it must be a place where prayer is fermented.

In the content, they were talking about the temple of God or what we call "church" in our days. But again; let's not forget that there is the dimension of the temple where we not just talking about a place we go to fellowship but you in person being the temple. Our bodies are the temple of God (*see 1 Corinthians 6:19-20*). If the principle of the temple of God being a house of prayer remains to be true, then we are supposed to be that house of prayer. In our days the spirit of God doesn't really dwells in a house built by man's hand but dwells in us as sons of God, and this reveals a dimension of prayer whereby your life become prayer. So in this dimension, is not about you praying whenever you can, but your life becomes a life of prayer.

Prayer has become the most difficult practice in our Christian journey. It has become so difficult for believers to spend time in prayer; that is why our prayer meetings are the least attended yet they should be the most attended since they are the source behind the manifestation of the power of God. Like I said before; if we will fail to manifest the power of God, no matter how fluent we can be, our message is empty. We become noise makers if there is no power, because the kingdom of God is not in words but in the demonstration of the power.

Prayer is what gives birth to the power we need to demonstrate the kingdom of God. If you are prayer less, you will never truly reveal and experience the possibilities of the kingdom of God. Be a prayerful person if you want to experience this resurrected life of Christ. It's true there are those who are prayer warriors, but in basic level we all as sons of God supposed to be prayerful. We will never succeed in the things of God unless we are prayerful.

Personally I value the quality of a church by its prayer meetings, because I understand that it is impossible to reveal the Kingdom of God with

His power and it's impossible to have the power without serious intimacy communion with God through prayer. Learn to prayer, invest in prayer if you are serious about experiencing this Greater Life.

Be very careful of who mentors you especially on the aspects of prayer. Remember, a baby doesn't take form at the time of birth but at the time of growth. Meaning who you are to be, is determined by who or what is helping you to grow. Many people even great preachers mentor other from the frustration of their limitations; just because they could not experience certain spiritual realities, they then turn to mentor others to believe it's an impossibility.

I once heard greater popular teacher of the Word saying people shouldn't be stress about praying long prayers now because Jesus has done everything for us. Yooh! Honestly I was discouraged, but then I started to look deeper into his life and I then understood why he believe long prayers are not important. In as much as he is a good teacher/preacher, I noticed that his congregation was dying of spiritual frustration. And honestly I couldn't understand why all these great teachings he's giving every now and again are not helping the people to live a Christ life as they should. I then noticed that there was no spiritual backup, meaning there was no demonstration of the kingdom of God in the ministry.

My beloveth! Never allow anyone or anything to discourage you in being prayerful. The Jesus we look up to and even read about from the scriptures was a man of prayer and to be more specific "long prayers". If Jesus being Jesus believed and relied on prayer, who are you to think you can succeed without prayer.

I personally encourage long prayers especially when praying in tongues. Remember when we speak in tongues we speak not to man but God, so if prayer is talking to God then it should be administered mostly in tongues. Paul once said he rather speak five words in language of man and ten thousand words in unknown tongues (*see 1 Corinthians 14:19*). Paul is revealing to us that it is more important to pray more in tongues than in language of man if you are talking to God.

When we pray in tongues, we are actually investing to increase our spiritual capacity to contain more of the things of the spirit. Be encouraged to pray as more as you can because only men who have travelled far enough in the spirit are entrusted with the mysteries of the Kingdom of God.

Paul once said he thank God that he can speak in tongues more than all those he was referring to (*see 1 Corinthians 14 :18*). Why would Paul thank God that he can speak in tongues more than some if it was of no spiritual importance? Your investment in the spirit determine what you can experience from God in terms of the spiritual realities.

I know this book is not about pray, but if we will lack pray we will never experience this resurrected life. So, be encouraged to pray more. Learn to pray as more as you can. Develop your prayer life if you are to experience more than what is normal.

And all this is for the resurrected life God is calling us into.

We are expected to live the spirit life in these physical bodies and execute the will of God here on earth as it is in heaven.

Arise and shine for the light has come! SHALOM!

PRAYER:

May this be your daily prayer for as long as you live!

CONFESS THIS PRAYER:

Father in the name of Jesus Christ, I am yours and You are mine.

Help my weakness and transform me to look more like You in every detail of my life.

May You alter my desires to be Your Desires Oh God

Help me to live Your Life with Faithfulness

And keep me in Your presence so that I can fulfil Your Will

Now and Forever

AMEN!

YOUR LIFE SHALL NEVER BE THE SAME AGAIN!

STAY BLESSED!

SCRIPTURE TO STUDY AS YOU DEVELOP YOUR PRAYER LIFE AND LIVING THE RESURRECTED LIFE:

A. Develop your prayer:

1. First know that it is the will of God for you to pray without ceasing - **1 Thessalonians 5:16-19**
2. Pray the Will of God - **Matthew 6:10**
3. Know that God is always listening and ready to respond to your call - **Jeremiah 33:3**
4. When you pray believe that you have already received from God - **Mark 11:24**
5. Be honest and open with God all the times with no doughs   - **James 5:16**
6. Prayer always works hand in hand with Faith - **Matthew 21:21-22**
7. You will always need prayer in every case or situation -**James 5:13-14**
8. Come before God with confidence - **Hebrews 4:16**
9. Keep pushing even when the flesh is not willing - **Matthew 26:41**
10. Let prayer be your life - **1 Thessalonians 5:17-18**

B. Living the resurrected life:

1. First acknowledge that you have no life of your own apart from the life of Christ.

2. Acknowledge the fact that there is a greater life than what you have experienced – **John 10:10**

3. Know that if you were baptized in the name Jesus Christ, there is an expectation by God for you to life the resurrected life – **Romans 6:4**

4. Living a resurrected life confirms that we belong with Christ – **Romans 8:9**

5. Live and walk by the spirit – Galatians 5:25

6. Change your desires to be heavenly – **Colossians 3:1-2**

7. We prove our origin through living this resurrected life – **John 3:6-8**

8. Love is evidence of the spirit life – **1 John 3:14**

9. Don't be lovers of pleasure – **1 Timothy 5:6**

10. The spirit life is maintained by Christ – **John 6:57, 1 Corinthians 10:3-4**

11. Complete surrender is the key to spiritual service – **Romans 12:1**

12. Seek to grow in the things of the spirit – **Ephesians 4:15, 1Peter 2:2**

YOUR ARE FREE TO SEND YOUR COMMENTS ON THIS BOOK AND HOW IT HAS TRANSFORMED YOU LIFE ON THE FOLLOWING DETAILS:

- liquiblozom@gmail.com
- +27 79 958 9240 (WhatsApp)
- Also to any of our social media platforms

We look forward to hear from you.
Stay Blessed!

CONNECT WITH MELUSI T NTOMBELA

LIVING A RESURRECTED LIFE

This book is an invitation to a place of the true manifestation of the power of God. It's an invitation to a reliable fellowship with God and have evidence of the possibilities of His kingdom.

The gospel of Jesus Christ is good news, but what makes it good news is the revelation of the power behind the gospel. If we have no revelation of the power of God; the gospel will not be good news.

MELUSI T NTOMBELA is a teaching pastor, a founder and senior pastor of Age Of Greater Glory International Ministries and the CEO of MT Mystery Ministries. Originally born in the kingdom of Eswatini but currently living in South Africa.

One who received the grace to have his eyes opened to see and understand the mysteries of God.